The Great Sweetening

Life After Thought

By

Jan Frazier

JanFrazierTeachings.com

Author of

When Fear Falls Away: The Story of a Sudden Awakening
(Weiser Books, 2007)

The Freedom of Being: At Ease with What Is
(Weiser Books, 2012)

Opening the Door: Jan Frazier Teachings on Awakening
(eBookIt, 2012)

Published by eBookIt.com
http://www.eBookIt.com

ISBN-13: 978-1-4566-2945-8

Table of Contents

And sometimes there is the expression in someone's eyes,

or in the voice, or in the letters on the screen,

that says something is happening there.

Something radical.

The great sweetening is taking over.

Being a Smart Animal

Once upon a time there was a creature endowed with a fine mind, and also with sense receptors that were sweetly attuned to the surrounding world and to its own delightful body. This intelligent and feeling creature could pick up sense impressions and savor them, without seeking to understand or to name or categorize any of what was smelled or heard or seen or touched or tasted. Life was a bounty.

Sometimes the excellent mind would become engaged, processing impressions in a way that was handy. The mind was a curious processor, taking a particular kind of non-physical delight in drawing connections and conclusions. This was one of the pleasures of being a smart animal. The mind would notice similarity between one tall growing thing and another, and pronounce them *trees*. The sensation in the mouth was pleasing, the tongue and lips and saliva cooperating to produce a new thing, a word. Thus it became possible for one of the creatures to say to another, "Tree," in the absence of the growing thing itself, and for the two of them to form in their minds a picture in common. This picture felt almost as real as an actual tree, notwithstanding the absence of the feel under the touching fingers, the distance traveled up with the eyes, the sound of the leaves in the wind, the smell of the fallen leaves decomposing at the feet of the tree.

It came to pass that the name for a thing, which lived only in the mind and the mouth, took on the appearance of reality itself (which continued to be discernible by the senses only). The word *good* came into being, and also *bad,* and they too seemed to name something real (even though what they named existed in the mind, not in the world).

Increasingly attuned to the mind's version of reality, the intelligent animals created a *self*, to go with each of their bodies. No one noticed that each evolving self had no independent existence, outside of a mind thinking it into being. No self was discernible by the senses (unless you counted the person's body, which everybody knew was a very minor portion of a self).

This self appeared to need maintenance and protection. It seemed to have a continuity across experiences, which made time seem like a real thing. The past seemed real because of the mind's ability to revisit something that had happened, and the future seemed real because of the mind's ability to fantasize and to worry about something that had not happened.

More and more, the mind's picture of things was mistaken for reality itself. The mind-made self learned to invent problems to fret over, having usually to do with wishing life were other than it was. The self and the problems were so compelling that the intelligent creatures came to live not in the real world but in their heads.

The problems spread over the earth, taking up much more room than the trees and the rocks, the continents, and even the buildings and cars. Then the smart animals, sinking under the weight of their mind-made problems, used those same minds to try to fix the problems.

Alas, they were unable to see the only real problem. Which was this: if the mind has created the problem, it cannot hope to fix it.

Then somebody said – *Why don't we just stop making the problems? Why don't we stop living in our heads?* And so they did, all on a single day. Profoundly relieved, with bounteous energy freed up, they turned their creativity and love to caring for one another and their dear planet. And they all lived peacefully ever after.

The Truest, Realest You

I found a door I hadn't known was there. It was like entering into another dimension, only this wasn't science fiction, or a dream, or delusion. It was just plain true. There had been a door all along, in the room in which life-so-far had taken place, fifty years of it. Suddenly I turned and looked in a direction I'd never looked before, and a door I'd never seen was slowly opening, waiting for me to step through. I stepped.

It was like that scene in *2001: A Space Odyssey,* where the monolith that was buried millennia ago is now, newly uncovered, about to be touched for the first thrilling time by the rays of the sun, which will set in motion something revolutionary. The dramatic opening notes of *Also Sprach Zarathustra* will play, lest you miss the significance of the moment. The monolith shape is reminiscent of a door, a tall shiny black door, standing free of any walls.

But this – this door that opened in my awareness – is not science fiction, or a movie. It's a plain-old life, *my* ordinary human life. Anybody's life. Only stepping into the newfound space causes life-ever-after to have nothing plain-old about it.

The thing is (and I have yet to get over this), what I saw vividly was that the door had been there all along. How could I have missed it? How could we *all* – humankind, that is – miss noticing the ever-present door? How is that possible? For years now I've been scratching my head about this.

We think that our ideas about life, about ourselves, are reality itself. This is the cause of our suffering. Our

mental pictures have us so convinced of their
objectivity, their legitimacy, that it doesn't occur to us
to consider another possibility.

We live all our lives contained in a room of our own
making. Reality is what it is: mentally unfiltered life
occurring, moment by moment, one day followed by
another. We are there for it. But what we live in is our
interpretations of things. Our elaborate and pain-
inducing stories. Meanwhile, uninterpreted life goes
on, at a great distance from our consciousness.
Trapped in our minds, we miss life itself – the real
thing.

When the door is noticed, it's an invitation to step
outside the mind-made room into actual life:
immediate, sensory, unprocessed, unresisted *life*.
What encounters this life is plain consciousness. Not
the stories, the beliefs, the history that we bundle
together into a self that needs asserting and
defending. When consciousness encounters life, all is
profoundly well. Maybe even fun. At the very least,
peaceful.

Yes, even when life dishes up a big challenge. There is
unending peace and well-being. Because there is no
resisting, no mental processing.

It's a stunner.

Why don't people see this door? Why didn't I? To step
through its opening is to leave behind many cherished
things: grudges, wounds, ambitions. Identity. Dignity,
self-esteem, familial pride. Anger and hope. Defenses.
So many things that we hold to ourselves, like
comforting clothing. The irony is terrible, as all of this
is what causes us to suffer. To miss the real thing!

Meanwhile, we point to life and declare *it* the cause of our misery. So why bother noticing the door, when we can't bear to consider the idea that we ourselves (not life) are the makers of our torment? Anyhow, it's impossible to imagine that it could be otherwise.

This *must* be science fiction, you may be thinking – that it could truly be otherwise. That's what I would have thought, had someone proposed such a thing to me. Anyhow, I don't recall really noticing there was a door there. I seem to have fallen through the opening. I looked around and saw the familiar world . . . only vastly changed. Well, it was the same world, the same life. But *I* was utterly different inside.

* * * * *

It seems to have to do with perspective. Stumbling through the door separating our usual way from the alternate one is about looking *at* something you've previously looked *through,* like a lens. You're looking from a different place. Things don't look the same from this point of view.

It's like looking at a room, at the structure you've occupied your whole life, *from the outside,* whereas before, you've lived entirely *in* it. Only before, you didn't realize this was a room you were in. (Let alone that there was an "outside" the room.) You always thought this room was just . . . *reality.* Having no idea that you had constructed the place, using your ideas about things.

But now, you're looking *at* the construction, from some point located outside of it. The simple fact of having relocated your perspective has changed everything. Among other things, it has altered your ability to suffer.

But hardly anybody is aware of this phenomenon. Even rigorous spiritual seekers often are unaware of the nature of the change that has to occur in order for suffering to stop. Mostly, it's believed that the necessary change has to do with trying harder to be at peace, to quiet the mind, or come up with a more "positive" or "spiritual" set of beliefs, or to heal from some emotional wound.

All of that effort occurs inside the room (however spiritually decorated it might be). This has been likened to rearranging the furniture inside the prison cell. Moving around the deck chairs on the Titanic.

All the while this earnest effort is taking place, there is the enduring impression that you *are* your history, your beliefs, your pain, your spiritual practices. The sense of who you are (that room you're in) is constructed of these things. This impression of *you* turns out to be the *only* problem – that you mistake all of this for what you are. As if there were not, within your very existence, a vast spaciousness that partakes of none of that familiar self-definition.

And so suffering continues.

The room each of us occupies appears to be the whole reality. What each of us calls "my life." Yet around this apparent reality, literally *inside* us and present in every moment we live, is something very like space. It goes everywhere you go. You can sense it in any moment your attention is *here*. When you cease believing your thoughts. When you aren't resisting anything.

It isn't necessary for the mind to be quiet. All that matters is that you not listen to what it's saying, as if it were true. One of the primary building materials of the room that seems to be *you* is the mental stream. When you invest in your thoughts, you are laying down cinderblocks and smearing mortar between them, busily keeping yourself feeling okay about yourself with more and better cinderblocks. If you look under your feet as you work, you'll see what you're standing on. The floor (previously nailed into place by you) is made of the unquestioned assumption that if you believe a thing to be true, then it must be. Focused as you are on keeping the walls solid, you don't even *realize* this is the underlying structure of your sad existence. That's why it endures. As far as you know, it's simply a fact. Not only real but *necessary*, to keep you "secure." (With security like that, who needs terrorists?)

Meanwhile, on the other side of the light-blocking walls, the vast spaciousness goes on forever, in every direction. *Inside* of you. (The real you.) Within ordinary consciousness, palpable in this moment's stillness. Just on the other side of the invisible door.

Who knew?

Space does not suffer. It does not compute time, or a self. It sees the movement of thought the same way it sees clouds forming and unforming themselves.

If you look around at the structure of the room and its furnishings, you will see all of your formative experience, how your relationships define you, the contents of your value system, your goals, your work life, the things you're admired for, the stuff you're lousy at. You'll see your image in a mirror and how you feel about that. Your ethnicity, gender, sexual preference. Your name. The atmosphere in the room is your earnest attempt to improve one thing and another, in yourself (and maybe in others). And so much more, of course. There could not be a sufficiently exhaustive list of what can be found inside the room. It's a wonder anybody can breathe, or move. (Did you ever wonder why it's hard to really rest?)

Everybody has (is) a room. It comes with the territory of being a person. The question is, where do you locate your *self*? Are you able to look *at* the construction, to see that it's something you've assembled? Or are you convinced there's nothing else to you but the apparent reality inside your head? For that, of course, is the location of the room.

Entirely inside your head. (Don't expect the ego to warm to this idea.)

The question is, what are you that is *not* made of thought?

When you're outside the room, looking at it, what is it you're looking *with?* It's not ordinary thought, is it? It's more like light. It's consciousness itself. You're simply aware. There is no emotional quality to the looking. Nothing personal about it at all. No investment, no angst.

If you allow yourself to grow quiet and still for a few moments, and you feel around inside your body, inside your awareness, to see if you can tell whether you're alive, right now – if you do that . . . sure enough, you can tell. Yes! Alive! Aware!

How can you tell? What did you use to know that?

That "knower," that looker, is not inside the claustrophobic room where suffering thrives. It's in

that vast space. Yet it is, surely and truly, within *you*.
It's the truest, realest you.

Radically Transient

We think of ourselves as stable entities that move through time, as if time were a medium. Things happen that we observe and respond to. We do things. We're affected by what happens. Though life changes us, there appears to be a rough continuity of self, recognizable from day to day, year to year, as the identity moves through its influences.

The impression of a stable self, a given persona that sustains over time, occurs when a person *thinks*. It is never directly *experienced* in a moment of life.

It's one thing to think about self, to revisit beliefs and knowledge, to reflect on a prior time or a projected future, visualizing the influences of experience on the self. It's another thing altogether to experience momentary life. The direct sensation of whatever life du jour is dishing up – this thing that's happening right now, when you're tuned in, really doing it, feeling, engaged, alert – *that* is the only mode in which a person directly senses that there's someone here. A moment of lived life is the only environment in which you can sense a self existing.

It's only when the mind gets hold of life, either during or in the aftermath, that the other thing happens – the appearance of there being an ongoing self that moves through time (as if time were a real thing).

The past and the future cannot be experienced. They can only be mentally processed. Past and future exist only in the form of thought. Time literally has no existence independent of our thinking about something "in" time. Understanding about a person's conditioning, belief systems, values – these can "come to life" only as mental activity.

When attention is on the immediate (whatever the particular "content" may be), when there is no resistance in the picture, the experience is that you *are* the moment. You don't notice this consciously, maybe, but something in your vital self feels it. There is not a "you" having an experience. Nothing of you exists apart from the unfolding moment that you are "in" – that you literally *are*.

The mind (having no reference points outside mental activity) cannot possibly understand this. Deeply invested in the mind's busily-constructing image of a self, the ego balks at the suggestion that the self has no existence in reality. A person would do well to rest from the effort to convince the ego-mind of the fact of the matter.

The self each of us appears to be – the mind-generated picture – is not something that's ever directly experienced. It is not *experience-able,* because who we think of ourselves as being exists only as a fabulously complicated thought, a hodgepodge of memory and belief and angst and desire.

We can't stop ourselves from thinking, from reflecting on what just happened, from looking back over life and seeing what's taken place over the years. It's natural to observe trends, to notice change, to learn from experience, to wonder what's ahead. This is not an argument for trying to stop any of that normal (and sometimes useful) human tendency.

But seeing that mental content has no independent existence in reality does help restore attention and vitality to what's here right now, to what's happening in the immediate scene – which is where life occurs. However true or valid or useful any stream of thoughts may appear to be, anything that's produced by the mind is at a remove from life itself. This is very useful to see.

This, here, is where we exist. Momentary experience is an order of reality apart from anything the mind can come up with, including its effort to define *you*. However astute or compassionate the observations of the mind, they are at a necessary distance, at a discerning remove, from life itself. When you feel yourself *be,* because you are laughing with a friend, or feeling really sick, or engaged with a little child who's telling you a story, or you're running full tilt, or sitting in the sun, or painting a wall, or digging in the earth, or singing a song that is breaking your heart – when you are, in short, really alive, feeling that you are *here,* this moment, having this very experience, this form that life is taking right now – *that* is reality, your reality, all you have (or ever will have) of life itself. Whatever else there is – all the rest of it, every scrap of remembered or anticipated life – is of a different order of things. It does not exist except when you *think* it into being. However much pleasure it may bring, or however much worry it has the power to generate, it remains the case that it has no independent existence outside the mind.

You (as you are used to thinking of yourself) do not exist except when you think yourself into being.

A person's only true existence is here and now, in actual encounter with what-is. We are radically transient, constantly in flux. We only appear otherwise when we think about ourselves. When the impression of being a stable entity is allowed to dissolve, when the mind-made image of self ceases to be a point of reference, then life is lived. Life is ever new, as we ourselves are.

The Three-Sided Structure We Live In

This is not a method. It is a way of looking at what occurs. It's looking at the level on which the change takes place, when a person goes from limited and fearful and mind-bound to utterly free, not just for a flickering instant but for keeps.

In order for the old way to hold itself together, certain things must appear real. They must be believed in as substantial. If the underpinnings of any one of them are knocked out, meaning that thing no longer seems real, the others will not be able to hold up and will also collapse. As soon as any one of them goes, the light floods in. You can visualize it as a three-sided structure, similar to a pyramid, the sides leaning in toward one another, supporting one another, coming to a stable point at the top.

The three are belief in time, belief in a self, and belief in thought. The base conscribed by the three forms the sense of reality.

This model is not something that can be entered. Thinking about it is not going to get you anywhere. You are already inside it. A person lives within this three-sided structure, feet on the ground of what seems real, in the dark.

There is the impression of a flow of time, of the past being accessible, via memory, and of the remnant influences of history on who you have become. The things you haven't gotten over continue to occupy your awareness in the present. The prospect of things getting better, or at least different, or possibly much worse, keeps the future alive. Hope and expectation and fear make the future seem like a real thing. The fact that change is inevitable, that aging occurs (not to mention death), and that anything could happen next – all of this keeps the eyes on the time that hasn't happened yet but sure looks as though it will.

The self that you appear to be seems to be a stable entity, recognizable and continuous. You appear to continue being here. What you do and your physical traits seem to have something to do with who you are. How others see you contributes to your sense of self. When things happen, they seem to happen "to" you, or you may bring them about. (*Somebody* did it.) You care what happens because of its effect on you. You "hold" yourself, with a wish to keep yourself safe and in a good light. You certainly do seem real.

If you sometimes see the unreliability of your ideas about things, how subject to change they are; even if you can sometimes distance yourself from the activity of your mind, the great part of the time you live inside your head, as if its story-line and imagery were accurate representations of truth. The thoughts you think have everything to do with determining your emotional reality. When you are absorbed in thought, you do not experience the now.

Time seems real. You seem real. Your thoughts seem to be on the same plane of reality as something sensory and immediate.

It is easy to see how the three support one another, how each depends upon the apparent reality of the others. They all keep each other going. There cannot be a "you" unless it occurs over time. The appearance of time, of a self, can occur only when you *think* about these things (when you remember what happened yesterday, or anticipate what might happen tomorrow; what kind of person you have always been, how you imagine people see you). The idea of wanting to change yourself: that is a thought, and it presupposes a continuity of a self, over time.

The three beliefs are operating, in one way or another, in just about any expression of the ego you can point to. You can watch it happen. (If you keep your eyes open.) You can learn a huge amount about how it all functions.

This is not pointing to some kind of method. It's just a way of seeing what happens. You are not in charge of what happens. There *is* no method.

Time, self, and thought are a triumvirate. When one of the three ceases to appear real – when you suddenly get, like a smack upside the head, that time does not exist, that this moment is it, is really actually *it* . . . or, when you cannot locate yourself, either because some devastation has crumpled the ground beneath your feet into some unrecognizable terrain, or into air through which you are plummeting, or because you have the shock of realizing you have made yourself up, all your life, or because you have a fleeting experience of being one with all-that-is . . . or, when you get the utter artificiality, the cut-and-dried inventedness of every thought you have *ever* had, and you see that the apparent "truth" of a given thought still does not bring it into the arena of present-moment reality as experienced in your viscera – when any one of these three walls of the pyramid in which you live has been brought to collapse, to detach from its fellow uprights, the others will go in short order.

This is not a method. You cannot take this and run with it. It doesn't work that way. We are not in charge of bringing about the demolition.

But. There is a reason to bother laying this out, inventing this possibly illuminating diagram of the three-sided windowless room inside which a person lives. To look at the way all three parts have to be there to keep the thing stable, to see how any one of them collapsing means the game is over, and there is light.

When you are watching yourself live, now, seeing how it all functions, how you hold together the nightmare you presently experience as your life . . .

Oh, you may be thinking, *it isn't really a nightmare.* It's not so bad, you think.

Later on, when you are looking back, you will see how bad it was, when you were reassuring yourself things were tolerably okay.

As you are observing how it is now, see – as moments are actually occurring, being lived, experienced – see how much relies on the triumvirate. How the sense of self keeps upright and strong. How readily it takes offense, feels under siege, how hard you work to repair any damage. How time keeps on seeming real, the hope for the future (that you'll get better, heal, wake up), the lament for the past. See how the mind keeps pitching balls, how automatic is the impulse to swing. The satisfaction of a good idea, the right understanding. The desolation of the idea that turned out to be bad, and how at sea you feel when you don't understand something, or turn out to be mistaken. The comfort of belief systems. Stories. Watch how it feels when your good idea crashes into somebody else's negative impression of it. How personally it is all taken.

Watch how it all holds itself together, how one depends upon the other.

You cannot make the walls of the pyramid fall. But you *can* see how they hold themselves up, and that you are not a passive participant in their maintenance. It is productive to do this.

And you are not in charge of whether or not the earth shifts, what brings about the great buckling underneath your feet.

When Everything Changed

Early on, there were the moments it would dawn on me, like something light coming to land on my arm, that suffering was gone. This was before I understood what had happened. All I knew was that whatever had been able to twist into a knot no longer was here, no longer functioned. It was the *absence* of something that was coming to me, the utter goneness of a capacity. It was a capacity I seemed to have been born with, so innate did it appear to be. I had no memory of a time before it.

Now, at intervals – at first many times in a day – it would grow quiet inside, and I'd look and that familiar thing wouldn't be there.

It was because something would occur in my day, something that once would have set me off, or startled me, or got my dander up, or got me worrying. That kind of thing would happen, but no reaction. And I'd go looking: *where is it?* Where was the tension in the belly, where was the scowling face, the grasping for control? Nothing. A flood, then, of recognition: *this again*. It's not the way it was. I'm not the way I was.

Then the next flood: relief. Then the next: gratitude. Joy. Amazement.

Sometimes, a wondering: *how could this be?* And *where did it come from?*

But never once was there the thought that the old way might come back. There would have been no place for it to get in, to reinsert itself into the machinery.

The thing was, I hadn't ever really understood how much pain I'd been in. I thought I had some idea. We do think we know; we have a vivid sense of how much we're bothered. Forlorn, stressed, angry, afraid, guilty, conflicted. It gets our attention. But it wasn't until it was altogether gone that I got the extent of how bad it had been. It was like I could breathe for the first time in my life. Like I could really, finally, rest. And laugh. I was so light. I didn't feel in any sense my old familiar weighed-down self. My trying-so-hard self.

It was a shock, looking back, seeing how I had done myself in, for all those years. How I had done it all to myself.

Why would we do such a thing?

Oh, but we don't realize we're doing it. Or if we do, we don't suppose there's any choice in the matter. It's only *after* that it becomes so clear.

After: when the seeing has happened.

In the beginning, joy is like a geyser, because of the contrast with before. You can't tell yourself *wow* enough times. But then it all begins to feel just normal. You forget you used to hit yourself on the head with a hammer. The contrast isn't vivid anymore. You just live. Joy is like an established fire: steady and warming, but no big crackle and impressive flame.

If you go looking, though – if you sniff around for remnants of the old misery – you can't find any closet doors to open. The closets are nowhere to be found. It's all different.

The Past Is a Sheer Cliff Just Back of Your Heels

The past is a sheer cliff just back of your heels. It's all down there, so far below that when you look over your shoulder and down, you can barely make out details of any of the rubble. The moment before this one is down there, tumbled in with the wreckage of yesterday, last week, last year, and the first day of high school. It's all the exact same amount of *past*.

You are standing in a place that is just the size of your shoes. You will never move. You only seem to move. Your feet cannot be anywhere but this now.

The mind is able to move. The feet are here while the mind is twenty years ago, or next week, or maybe-someday, or an hour ago. The feet and heart are here. The past has all dropped behind you, gone as gone can be, but the mind can't quite believe the utter goneness. It cannot see the utter impossibility of reconsidering, of remaking what has happened. The uselessness of trying to make it okay that it happened the way it did.

Consolation is as useless as regret. The thing about the past is that it is *gone*. And that it is a fact. These are the only useful things to see about the past.

The future doesn't exist. Only one thing is real: *now*.

Only when the past is allowed to be a mere fact, only when the future isn't counted upon, does it become possible to take a deep breath and actually occupy the present.

This is why the mind is so significant. Why seeing that the mind isn't *you,* isn't life, is key to being here now. Whatever the mind creates for content is at a remove from immediate life. Suffering is created in the mind. You can't stop the mind. But you can step outside and watch it create content. The reason you can do this is that there is more to you than your mind. When you step outside and see what it's doing, you are in reality. You are here, now. You are experiencing the moreness of yourself, the hereness of yourself. You are able to see, from here, that the mind cannot do you harm so long as you don't live inside it, believing its rendering of reality.

What people tend to do, when they want to end the mind's torment, is to try to use the mind's own arguments to vanquish itself, to reason with itself. This will never work. Just let the mind go on muttering to itself. Walk outside the room where it's going on.

It's peaceful out there.

After a while of doing this, when you get to where you can readily step outside, you'll find that the mental content fades from color to black-and-white. After a while, when you stop living within it, you'll feel your feet where they *are.* You'll feel your heart. You'll smell the air. You'll face the present reality, whatever it is, with all your resources (including, by the way, your useful *mental* resources). Your attention will be on what you're doing. You'll forget there is even a past back there, that there's a pile of rubble far below, just back of your heels. It's all just what happened, exactly how it happened. Nothing more. You'll find acceptance easy, natural. You won't be afraid of the future, or try to make it a certain way. You'll forget it's even coming, because all of your attention will be right here.

You're alive. Welcome to your life.

A Child Again

Living awake feels like being in a child's story, a simple story about a simple thing. The restoration to innocence, to the time before time, with no possibility of harm. Once-upon-a-time. The garden of Eden.

That's what it feels like. A person who has awakened feels like a little kid. Everything is fresh and new, every ordinary thing. How good it feels to brush your hair! How the trees look moving in the wind. The sensation of urine releasing.

You tilt your head at people's complaints and worries, trying to understand. The effort to wring meaning out of every life episode, to pronounce it good or bad. Your heart breaks (but not for long).

You do remember what it feels like to be caught up in problems (your own, your wife's, your child's, the country's), to have it all matter so much, everything riding on one outcome or another. What it's like to be convinced time is a real thing, to be tormented by its apparent brevity, haunted by aging and death. But now, you could just sit the livelong day, never read another newspaper, work on another project. Things smell good. You move from one savoring to another. The way light plays on a stranger's face. It's like when you were a kid, enthralled with the feel of warm sand falling through your spread fingers.

The pleasure of awareness is exquisite like that sand. There's absolutely nothing going on, and how can *nothing* feel so substantial? What could be more delicious than this, just feeling this moment? How did you ever imagine any of that other stuff mattered so much?

Like a little child, you care nothing for time, nothing for people's expectations. The world, the physical world, is the entire miracle. And here you are, in it.

Look! See, smell, touch! Oh, taste! Tuna! Garlic! Ice cream! Wine! Coffee! Lips!

* * * * *

Before a child has been outfitted with the adult-made lenses we all learn to look through, before becoming entrenched in the ideas of things, of right and wrong; before categories arrive on the scene, before expectations, somebody's idea of self-esteem, dignity – before, even, the name for a thing – there is direct apprehension. Encounter. There is feeling. No intervening mental filter. No urgency for an inner narrative.

This is what you are restored to at awakening, when the self you thought you were ceases to enthrall. Names for things are still there, retrievable. It's still possible for thinking to occur. But only when you want it to. Thinking no longer runs the show, the constant noise of it. Thought serves at the pleasure of what you have discovered yourself to be: consciousness itself.

Anything mental is secondary, if it's there at all. You have entered an existence made of primary experience – felt, sensory life, this moment. There's no distance between you and what you're aware of. You *are* what you experience. You and the moment are the same thing. This is the all-that-is.

The norm is awareness of what-is. This living consciousness is here for each episode of reality but does not mutter to itself about what it means. There is no spawning of opinion, fear, desire.

Often you are bewildered, the way a child is, at how people seem to be. No longer playing by their rules, you have to work a bit to remember what it feels like to be that way.

(Who is the grown-up here?)

But the almost universal way of being a person, which you can't help noticing, has trouble holding your attention. You keep getting absorbed in the way the fabric feels against your arm. The airiness in your mouth when you sing. The world, you keep discovering, is constantly *here*. It's what you find when life has finally stopped being about *you*. Even with all its apparent problems, existence is entirely miraculous.

Homesickness

Maybe there is such a thing as existential homesickness. A loneliness in the bones, seldom acknowledged, even to self. The sense that something has been lost, forgotten. Wanting to find the way home, but no idea of what direction to head in.

It's no wonder that when the machinery of suffering has fallen apart, and the mind has grown quiet, the feeling is that you've come home. Home has found you – which is often the impression, since you hadn't necessarily been trying to find your way there, not consciously anyhow. Or maybe you had been, but now you see you'd been looking in the wrong places.

All you know is, you no longer ask anything of life. There is not the remotest dissatisfaction. Whatever you've longed for is here, already. You can rest – finally, totally rest. Effort is like a sickness you have recovered from.

You look around you, and weirdly, none of the externals have changed. This observation is instructive. You see that your unhappiness never was, after all, caused by circumstance and event, the way you supposed.

Everywhere you go, you are home. Nothing is alien, or threatening. Even the familiar is utterly new. And yet also home.

You have lost interest in yourself. In what you used to think of as your problems. Your painful history. You no longer feel like the center of your universe.

It doesn't occur to you to balk at anything. Hope does not start up, or expectation. Or disappointment. You don't care whether you're thought well of. You take refuge in nothing, because nothing is threatening, or distressing.

How can this feel like home, familiar in that deeply restful way, when so much of how you used to function is simply gone? You don't feel like *you* anymore. Clearly this is new terrain, the goneness of all of the familiar reactivity and ambition and angst. And yet somehow, it's familiar. Something in you always knew this alternate possibility was here. This other way, this peaceful way, that underlay all that once seemed inevitable.

Because you are no longer a project for yourself (to maintain, improve, defend, console), your concern is for others. People and animals. Animals just live (which is now the case for you as well). People, you realize, wander around terminally homesick. Whether or not they are conscious of that, or understand what it's about. You know that if any one of them, even a happy, well-balanced person, were to suddenly stumble into this that is home, all that has absorbed them before would turn pale. Many are *not* happy and well-balanced. You see yourself in them. You know what it feels like to be sick with effort.

Plummeting and the Terror of Peace

Someone spoke of feeling panic when contemplating the prospect of absolute peace, the radical dropping into all-is-well. Others, hearing, laughed a nervous little laugh, a recognition. It seemed to be an anxiety they well understood.

Is this universal, or at any rate widespread? I think so. Way down there, beneath the desire for perfect ease, is the worry that if you let down your guard, drop the vigilance, something bad will happen. Is that what the panic is about? Is it the dread of boredom? Or maybe it's knowing that real peace would be so delicious, the relief so gigantic, that you just couldn't bear the crushing disappointment if it didn't hold up, if something came in to wreck it.

Whatever it is, I have a vivid memory of feeling it.

I think it's almost a physical thing. Contemplating the radical resting place conjures an utter relaxation of muscle tension. (It must be why we so love sleep.) And *something* is holding you, supporting you. The ability to completely let go seems to require that there be something beneath you, some kind of bedrock (or bed). Gravity does its thing, and there's no place lower for you to go, no deeper letting-go possible. There's some ground of being that won't go away, that isn't subject to dissolution.

This must be why people gravitate toward faith.

So why the roomful of nervous laughter, when someone said that thing about being panicky at the prospect of pure peacefulness?

Maybe it's that deep down we suspect any impression of bedrock is illusory. (There *could* be an earthquake, or maybe we'd get stepped on.) Maybe we secretly know we're in freefall, with no idea where, or whether, there will be a landing. And even if there *is* a landing place, it might turn out to be a trapdoor. Maybe something in us knows that the visceral longing to completely rest, to let go all muscle tension forever, can *have* no ultimately reliable support.

But that doesn't mean we can't have what we want. What we want is rest. Radical okayness.

Is it possible to be in freefall with no muscles clenched? No clenched mental muscle wondering if you're about to smack into something, constantly picturing possible doom?

What we want isn't a solid resting place *per se*. What we want is not to be tensed up, not to fear what's coming, the unknown. What we want is to drop the vigilance. That can happen in freefall, which is basically just lying down in the air. That's what being awake is: plummeting, with no idea of what's down there, completely relaxed. Enjoying the ride.

In Rumi's Field

Rumi says that out beyond ideas of wrong-doing and right-doing there is a field. It's where you finally can lie down and rest. Where blessedness takes you in its arms.

What in human experience is beyond all ideas, past wrong and right, happy and sad, positive and negative? Where is there a place past the reach of meaning, judgment, story – any story at all?

All our lives, one story gets replaced with another one, a better spin, a way of accounting for something. We want to have bearings, always.

What is it to be without bearings – gladly, and not in desolation, or terror?

What is it to be simply here, alive, aware, feeling? No mental filters, no box, no category, myth.

Why do we make all of that structure, do all that meaning-making? We can't bear not to know. We can't stand to bow to the radical absence of control, to confront the terror of uncertainty. So we make religions, frames of reference, ideologies, family legacies. We give names to things, ourselves included.

All a way of coping with the vast emptiness, with brevity.

What's left when the artifice of meaning-making blows away in the storm of becoming free? What are you left with when everything's bowed to?

That field, where stories do not flower, beyond the reach of idea and judgment, beyond meaning-making: why are they laughing there? They laugh with relief. With exaltation, delight.

Virtue didn't get them there, nor striving, nor good intentions. Work didn't make a path to that field. Collapse did it, utter willingness to go into the dark, into the raw, terrifying absence of meaning.

Are you angry? Anger is never the real thing, ever. Anger is the armor. Underneath anger is the blind, furless, infant thing that has been poked and threatened and left to fend for itself.

Anger isn't the authentic thing. It lives on the surface. Pay no attention to it. Go into the dark below it. Touch the raw nerve. Bow to *that,* to the broken heart, the loss that's yet to be yielded to. Exhale into that grief, or you will be angry forever. Give yourself to the underlying pain, and anger becomes a distant memory, a bird gone over the horizon.

Why, in that field beyond right and wrong, are they dancing? Why don't they appear heartless? Why don't they believe in anything? Why has language abandoned their mouths?

They can see one another, but they cannot see themselves. When they reach to touch themselves, their hands go right through. They are free because there is no one to protect, to stand up for, assert, console, heal. Why would they need a story?

They did, for a time. They could not, then, imagine a time, a field, beyond that need. The need to feel okay about themselves, to justify and explain. The answer to fear was the search for safety. Security was the beloved. They lived in containers. For a time, there was that necessary consolation.

At some point the screws began silently, or noisily, to be backed out. The walls began to crumble, fall. Or to become transparent. Their "selves" no longer mattered to them. The surprise of it! Everything touched them but nothing *became* them. Nothing hard was held up to anything, like a shield. Their necks stayed bowed.

Why are they laughing? Have they forgotten about the aching world? Do they not care? They are laughing at themselves, for how seriously they used to take all of it.

A person can't decide to toss a story overboard. It will resurface, reassemble itself, insist itself back into a container to occupy.

Still, it's possible to *see* the story, to know it is artificial, to see its function is to protect, to hold away the unfelt thing. It's possible to sense the moment when the story's function grows thin, when its usefulness has been outlasted, and then – if the willingness is sufficient – it becomes possible to decline to scramble to do the story-maintenance. You can decline to scurry for tools and materials, thought patterns and definitions and memory. You can let yourself fall, feel, drop into the deepest abandon your weight can rush toward, down, down, without putting your hands out in the dark to feel for someplace to grab, without wondering where the bottom will turn out to be, or if you'll ever see the light of day again.

How did you get here, to this field full of tenderness, this warm grass, where change is unceasing, and yet this utter stillness? This joy without a name?

Resting from Mind-Caused Suffering

This is the terrible irony of the vast majority of human suffering: the thing that gives rise to it in the first place is then asked to alleviate it. The mind cannot relieve what it has brought about. But this is what we attempt to do.

Reality comes along, and the mind spawns some kind of story or image that brews anguish. Then *the same device* is uselessly enlisted in the pursuit of comfort, coping, escape.

When the entire thing could have been skipped.

Mired in its interpretation of reality, the ego-mind tries to talk itself into believing it will all be okay, or at least bearable, understandable. It tries to get "positive" thoughts to push out "negative" ones. (A thought is a thought, regardless of which end of the spectrum it's on.)

Once the mind gets hold of some piece of reality and interprets it, the interpretation becomes your "reality." You're stuck with relating to that thing in your head *as if it were life itself.* Meanwhile, the actual life occurrence (as it was before the mind got its sticky fingers on it) is still its same self, floating out there somewhere, forgotten.

Yes, it's possible to encounter reality without the mind automatically engaging. At the very least, it's possible (and greatly relieving) to observe the mind doing its thing, to realize the mental handling is at a remove from reality itself, and so to not take it very seriously.

In the face of something difficult, what happens when the mind isn't automatically pressed into service? Reality comes along, and you *feel* it (not *think* it) along every surface of your body. You allow it to enter you, without resistance. It's a physical thing, a felt thing. There is recognition of what's here. The mind is blessedly quiet – at least, the mind as it's usually pressed into service by the anxious, controlling ego. You can still perceive, recognize, understand. Awareness is alive and well. It's just that you aren't taking the usual next step of figuring out what you think of it, what it means for you. You don't rush to forming an opinion, a judgment, even a label.

The reason the mind usually starts up, in the face of a challenging development, is to protect the ego in some way: to launch a counter-attack, to fit what's happened into some kind of familiar (mind-made) pattern, to seek consolation. Inevitably, the mental activity generates painful emotion . . . which you then want to ease somehow. So you look for some positive (mental) spin to put on the thing, or you try to distract yourself with different thoughts (or booze or the computer).

But using the problem-causer to solve the problem is . . . well, a waste of time. It will do nothing to put you in touch with your deeper nature, which is entirely comfortable in the presence of reality.

When the mind is allowed to be still (or at least recognized for what it's trying to do), and whatever is happening in life is taken in all the way – which occurs naturally in the absence of mental filters, of resistance – then the feeling in the body may be deep. Possibly very painful. Then, very likely, you will move on. The reality of the situation will have registered. If you need to take action of some kind, or think in a way that's practical (as opposed to torment-inducing), you will do that. But you won't be burdened with the mental mess that has previously attached itself to every life challenge.

* * * * *

A person might think that having a quiet mind, losing interest in your dignity, losing ambition and pride, becoming detached from your history – that all of this might land you in an *unfeeling* condition, where nothing can touch you. It's true that you're on an even keel. You aren't stirred up like you once were, by every little thing that comes along. But when something real comes (not from your mind but from life itself), if it is painful you will feel it all the way into your bones. There is no impulse to protect yourself. Because you are not lost in thought *about* the thing, you sense reality directly. Of course you will feel!

When you stop using your mind like a shield, there's no distance between you and life. "You" and "it" are a continuity. (What do you think *nondual* means?) Yes, you can choose not to go there. Nothing says you must subject yourself to every available misery, just because it's there. You can decide how often to look at the news. Because when you do watch, you will surely take it in – the suffering of another person, or people – as if the pain were your own. You may prefer to be alone, to pay only a little attention to the larger situation, only as attention is called for.

But when you encounter something painful, either because you go there deliberately or because it's close to home, it will saturate you. There will be no protective shield. The mind will be like an open window: out of the way.

There's a difference between mind-caused suffering and pain that has no mediator, that's felt spontaneously, before you've had time to think about what it means to your ego. When mind-caused suffering has stopped happening, you still *feel*. There is tenderness, openness, love. It's just that it isn't in the name of holding you together. It isn't about "you." The heart breaks open in the face of a death. Love floods in, sadness, cherishing.

The mind does have a useful role in such a situation. In the aftermath of the death of a loved one, a purely cognitive process occurs around the edges of felt grief. The fact of the goneness of the beloved has to "get through your head," probably many times. In the morning when you wake, there is the remembering: *he is no longer here*. Many times it will come to you, *I will not hear her voice again*. There are ways our native intelligence collects data and reminds us of changes in the landscape, so we can adapt to the new situation. This is useful.

But what doesn't happen is the story-making. The attempt to rescue you from the pain of missing, of loving when there is no one there to love. There is no keeping a stiff upper lip, keeping busy. There is no counting of the blessings, no avoidance of the possibly difficult particulars – the unresolved, the disappointing. No consolation: *at least he lived a long life*.

You aren't at a distance from life. You haven't become tough, or aloof. It's just that you no longer run everything through a filter. It's that you're no longer at the mercy of the mind, whose primary mission used to be to protect you. To keep you feeling okay about yourself, your circumstances, your prospects.

Your mind no longer exists to hold together a self. Your self is not of interest anymore, so the mind can rest most of the time. When thinking is needed, it operates much more efficiently and clearly than before, when a virus had infected all its functioning, when virtually every mental movement occurred in the name of holding away perceived threats, plotting a better future, seeking relief.

Now the mind is a blessing, when it's needed. Handy, practical, creative. Direct and skillful, nothing wasted. Generating no emotion. Mostly, it sits off to the side, quiet. Your body, though, is alive. You feel, the way an open heart feels. Not a heart that can get its feelings hurt. Not a heart that needs protecting.

Your senses are alert, without judgment. It doesn't occur to you to drop things into categories: *I like this; I don't like that*. What-is overwhelms every other consideration. You rest in what-is. You are in opposition to nothing – not because you're in favor of it, but because it's real.

You feel incredibly alive. Peaceful.

How can this be? That you are both fully here and yet the old you has broken apart into bits, melted away? How is it that you are really here and yet not attached to any of it? Reality doesn't bounce off of you anymore. It enters you, passes through you. You feel it, but it leaves you. It leaves you unchanged. Life doesn't determine what you are, how you proceed. It doesn't leave you with a revised set of beliefs, or with the old ones cast in murky light. You don't *need* beliefs anymore.

You want nothing. But life is here, happening.
Sometimes it hurts. Sometimes there is a surge of joy.
You're really here for it, all of it.

The Really Real You

You want to be happy. That's the starting place –
everybody's starting place. The desire for happiness
and ease. Fulfillment. Certain things seem to be in the
way of that. Life as it unfolds seems to want you to
believe that the things between you and happiness are
the circumstances and events of your life, of the world
around you. So the tendency is to focus on fixing
those. All in the name of happiness, ease, fulfillment.

Then, if you are lucky, you figure out that the thing
between you and happiness is in here, not out there. If
you are not so lucky, you live your whole life focused
on the wrong thing. If you are like a good chunk of
humanity, this is the way it is. So sometimes you're
happy, sometimes you're not, but either way, the
degree of happiness is determined by circumstances
and events. The plus column and the minus column.

The day you figure out the location of the *real*
problem is a great day indeed. Even though the
relocation of the focus of attention can appear to
cause a whole new mess. The discovery that your
mind is completely running the show is a revelation
with potential to bring about a happiness that is
absolute. It can also drive you really crazy. Just
because you have fathomed the power of the mind
does not mean you can figure out how to find the off
switch.

Oh, but the adventure has really just begun. Don't lose
heart. It's a necessary torture to become acquainted,
maybe for the first time, with how you get your sense
of who you are. How you can hardly experience a
thing without automatically dropping it into the good
column or the bad. How hard it is to see through all

that to the actual physical world, the actual unencumbered moment.

But the torture doesn't last, at least not if you're willing to stay with this thing. The thing being this: noticing where your attention is, moment to moment. Just that.

The reason the torture eases is that little by little you begin to take your thoughts less seriously. They become features of the landscape, like trees. Including, and most especially, the thoughts about who you are.

What is starting to happen is that a new kind of awareness is leaking in through the previously impermeable unit that was your sense of what is real. You could say it's a new awareness, but really, it's only newly showing up. It's actually deeply familiar to you, deeply comforting, and here is where we get to the happiness that is not subject to event and circumstance.

Meanwhile, life is still going on, one event after another, circumstances all around you. But something in the middle of it all is starting to recognize itself. To know itself. It feels real. It feels more real, once in a while, than any of the outer stuff. It feels like *you* . . . only, not the you you thought you were. Not the you who is a certain age, who has these particular looks and physical condition. Not the you having this collection of experiences, this set of gifts and deficiencies and beliefs. Not the you who loves these particular people, animals, activities, places. Not even the you who wants to wake up.

Yet . . . it feels like you. The really real you. Being there, feeling that, you are stunned at the stillness. It may be fleeting. You may not trust it.

Trust it.

When you look at some other somebody, you sense the same thing in them. Even if they don't sense it in themselves.

Ten seconds later, your head is full of thoughts again, and you seem to be the person you always seemed to be before, and the problems of your life seem to be located out there. Again.

Don't worry. Expect this to take a while. Oh, it might not. It might just all go away in one deep beat of the heart. Then you would be very lucky indeed. But don't expect that, or wish for it. It's best not to expect anything.

Just notice where the attention is, right now. That's all.

After a while, you will notice that there is an experience (an event, a circumstance) that you are there for, that you are maybe even in the middle of, and yet (are you ready for a miracle?) you observe that it doesn't seem to affect you in the old familiar way. You don't drop it into any column at all. No opinion, no thought even. The thing just is what it is. Then you go on. The next thing comes.

You may notice that there is this unaccustomed feeling of ease riding around in your body. Something that feels deeply familiar, and yet it doesn't seem to have to do with who you always thought you were.

Sometime after another while has gone by, you may notice that you can't remember the last time you looked to outer things for happiness. You also can't remember having any thoughts lately, except thoughts serving some practical function. You notice that when you catch an image of yourself in a mirror, there is nothing there that gets dropped into the plus or the minus column. It's just a person, on a particular day, this particular moment.

A Locked Door

A door without a lock. A door without a lock that appears to be locked – that gives the impression of being un-openable. This is the human situation. The door has no lock on it. But if you ask someone aching to be free of the mind and its mischief why they are not free, they will probably say the door to freedom is locked and they need to find the key.

Only, the door is not locked. Of course, if you *think* there is a lock on the door – then, well, there is. (Thinking makes it so.)

Some time ago I was walking to lunch with a friend, in a city unfamiliar to both of us. She had spotted a restaurant earlier that appealed to her. We walked there and she pushed on the door. It did not open. *Oh darn,* she said. *I wonder why they're closed.* She pushed again, I guess thinking the door might be stuck. But no.

We were just starting to walk away, to look for a restaurant that was open, when someone inside came toward the door and pushed it open.

My friend (a spiritual seeker) looked at me and laughed at the metaphor. She thought the door was locked . . . so we could not, in fact, enter.

Lunch was delicious.

The thing is not to try to find the key to the locked door. The thing is to figure out why you have got yourself convinced there is a lock. But people spend their lives trying different keys: meditate, try this teacher, do yoga, try that teacher, repeat a mantra, memorize prayers, go back to the first teacher.

It's never what it looks like it is. You can count on that much. The problem is the angle you are looking from. Or the eyes you are looking with. Or the lenses you are looking through.

There is no lock on the door. If you start by realizing you've got the wrong impression about there being a lock, then you can finally rest from looking for the key. Redirect your attention to exploring how you give yourself (constantly) the impression that there's a lock on the door.

It gets better. When you wake up and the door you always thought was locked swings liquidly open, you sail through. If you think to turn around and look behind you, there is no door. Let alone a lock.

Being Conscious

Being conscious occurs in the now. (Even if your attachment to ego has ended, and you're conscious as the norm, consciousness is experienced *now*.) When you're conscious, you're aware of what's happening in the now: sensation in your body, what your body is doing, things directly observable in the immediate scene. Consciousness is neutral, unresisting awareness of present-moment reality. There are no mental filters, no inner narrative. Simply awareness of what is, right now.

Consciousness is attention. It's different from thinking. Thinking involves processing, labeling, visualizing, categorizing, projecting. It causes emotion. Attention is simple awareness. It's peaceful (whether or not the immediate scene looks peaceful).

If something is going on in your mind at the moment, being conscious means you're aware *that you're thinking*. That is, you are not "lost in thought." Something is happening in your mind, and you're aware of that. It's just the same as if you were using some other part of your body to do something: if you are using your hands to slice carrots, you're aware of that. You are paying attention to what you're doing, whether you're doing it with your hands or your feet or your mind.

Being *unconscious* means you're lost in thought, in the pictures and stories your mind is producing. You have entered the made-up content of your mind and are occupying it *as if it were reality itself*. Your ego is invested in this content as being real and important, and very likely as a result you are experiencing some kind of emotion (stirred up by the thinking). You have forgotten that all of it is the product of your mind (even if its content appears to be true or important). As a result, you are missing actual reality, what's happening in the now – *including that you are inventing the thoughts.*

During a period of unconsciousness, the content of thought has become a replacement reality. When you're unconscious, your ego is completely running the show. Nothing useful can occur in terms of spiritual insight or development. Awareness is not in the picture. Only egoic thought is occurring. The ego cannot possibly be used to get out of its own way. Only awareness can see in such a way to quiet the identification with egoic thought.

When you're driving away from home and suddenly you don't know whether you turned off the stove, it's because you were thinking about something besides turning off the stove when you turned the knob (if in fact you did). If you had been paying attention to what you were doing, when you did it, you would know for a certainty that the stove is now off. If in fact you turned it off, you were unconscious at the time. You were lost in the momentary replacement reality occurring inside your head. You literally "weren't there" when your hand turned the knob. You were occupying the movie or soundtrack your mind was producing at the time.

Being conscious doesn't necessarily mean your mind is quiet. It means if your mind is doing something, you're aware of that, rather than being lost in its content. The more you become conscious that thought is occurring, during the times the mind is active, the less the mind will run all the time on its own. The reason it runs non-stop is that you enter into its content *as if it were real.* You don't notice you're thinking. You notice what the thoughts are *about*. If you keep giving yourself the impression that the content of your thought is reality itself – *rather than observing that you are thinking* – then your ego gets the message that you really must keep thinking all the time, because not to do so would be dangerous. It would be threatening to the well-being of the ego, which seems to be *what you are*. Thinking seems to be crucial to "your" (the ego's) continued existence.

As soon as you notice that you are thinking – that you've been absorbed in the content as if it were reality itself – some of the steam runs out of the mental activity. It's only when you believe your thoughts are reality that painful emotions are generated.

Of course there's such a thing as useful thought, the kind that has nothing to do with keeping the ego going. Practical thought does not cause emotion. It is applied to a purpose: making a plan for a trip, studying a new language, figuring out how to repair something that's broken. (Of course, the ego can find all kinds of ways to get in an uproar while these episodes of practical thinking are occurring. Like getting mad at the broken thing, or becoming frustrated because you can't figure out how to fix it. In which case, unconsciousness has taken over. But it isn't inevitable that it will always do so.)

You cannot decide to be conscious more of the time. This is not something to be "practiced." (Spare yourself this cherished illusion.) In any given moment, either you're conscious (aware) or not (lost in thought). You didn't "decide" which to be; it just happened, in a spontaneous kind of way. Even so, probably it's the case that the more often you are conscious – the more often you are *really here*, and not suffering – the more consciousness will predominate, as a general trend. Each time you're thinking and you happen to notice that you're thinking, something potent has occurred. It's just that you aren't in charge of when that noticing happens. Nature will, as ever, take its course.

Really Alive

Assume there is more to you than the apparent. Become acquainted with the awareness that isn't the ordinary mind. If you leave the door open, it will come. Like an unexpected visitor, a stranger you've known all your life. An intimate whose face is being seen for the first time, with a voice you recognize, though you've never heard it before.

It's you, only it doesn't come with an armful of stories. It's you, minus the complaints, the unresolved, the projects, the dread of what's ahead. It's just content to be here. To stretch its legs into this moment. Into this very stillness, absent anticipation of the next thing.

Memory is there, if you go looking. But it doesn't visit you of its own accord. Or if it does, it's without the familiar weight, the acid, the pressure. Like watching a movie.

The awareness that isn't the ordinary mind is still. Willing. It's ready to be there for anything. It has no agenda. It's receptive. Curious. Profoundly de-personalized. Matter-of-fact, like a cat washing itself. It doesn't miss a thing. It doesn't process. It's just *there*, for whatever happens.

It's how you can tell you're alive. Really here.

Only strangely, you've disappeared. The you that got assembled in the familiar way doesn't seem to be in the picture. Yet there is awareness. Receptivity. Delight, even.

Where does the awareness reside? What generates it? What is it that can tell it's here?

But you are disinclined to linger very long over these puzzlings. After all, the light and shadow and color are in motion. Breath is moving in and back out again. The cat is washing itself. The snow is starting to fall. Something is always happening, and you are there for it. It enters you, you feel it, and then it passes all the way through, and out, as if you — as if awareness — were a window screen. Generous like that. Nothing grasping. The thing is allowed, felt. You are unchanged.

The next thing happens. Things just keep happening. You're really there for it. All of it. When death begins murmuring into your ear, you relax into its arms. Because you have really lived.

Or, what you could do is crawl inside your head and spend your whole life there, being rocked and tumbled and massaged by stories that you don't even recognize as stories. As if what the mind makes of life were life itself. You could miss it.

There's a reason little children don't understand about time. They are really alive. Briefly.

Paying Attention

Attention is everything. Being present – feeling your aliveness in this moment – has to do with what attention is doing. Normally, the focus on the moment has to do with its content: the thoughts being thought (as if they amounted to reality), the thing happening "out there" (the traffic, the other person talking), the thing you're doing (sitting at the computer, helping your child with homework, changing the tire).

The direct experience of what you *are,* at your essence, has to do with sensing attention itself. In a wakeful moment, if you have any experience of your "self," what you feel is awareness itself. Not your story, not your beliefs, not anything to do with desire or fear.

When beingness senses itself, what's happening is that attention is attending itself. Time has stopped. "You" have tapped into the utter stillness that is your deep nature. Only attention has access to this. Thought cannot reach it. All thought can reach is thoughts. (Which is related to why thinking the right thoughts, or mentally understanding some teaching, will never wake you up.)

Paying attention to what's happening right now, inside and outside yourself, within the field of your awareness (without regard for whether you like it or wish it were otherwise), is important not just because it attunes you to reality (which is momentary and immediate, and all you've ever got). It's important because attention is the doorway to sensing what you deeply are – which has nothing whatever to do with the "content" of the moment. It's just that by putting attention on what's here right now, including whatever is going on within (thought, emotion, physical sensation), you engage that faculty that is your deep nature, outside of thought. You have opened the door to a deeper kind of encounter than what thought has access to.

When you instead engage the faculty of thought by entering into its current production – that is, when you engage with the mind-made movie du jour *as if it were reality* – your attention is being spent on something that *is not real.* You are missing reality because you're believing the thought stream that's distracting you from the immediate, the physical, the perceivable. You cannot sense what you deeply are when you are "living" inside your head, because all that's engaged is thought (and whatever emotions it brings to life).

However (and this is significant), when you are giving attention to the *phenomenon* of thought – that is, when you notice *that you are thinking* – and this is very different from occupying the thought as if it were real – *then* attention has been engaged. Which is why there's no point in trying to stop or counter a particular bunch of thoughts, because when you do that, you have gotten into the ring with the thoughts themselves, as if their content were the important thing. The important thing is to see *that you are thinking,* and *that the thoughts are productions of your mind,* not reality itself. When you are able to see this, then the thoughts can go on muttering to themselves, and you won't get caught in them. You can shift your attention to what your body is doing, or what it's feeling like, or what's going on around you. Or if you do get re-involved in the thoughts, you can just look once again at the fact that you are thinking, and feel what it feels like to have attention be on the phenomenon itself, and how that differs from entering into the apparent reality of the thoughts.

That in you that is able to attend in this way is not caught up in thought. There, you can feel that there is more to you than thought.

Your thoughts cannot ensnare or harm you as long as you continue to see that they are made up, that they are not the same as reality but are productions of your busy mind. If they can't harm you, there is no need to change them or get into a wrestling match with them.

Stop asking "Am I awake?" or "Will I wake up?" or "Am I having the desirable kind of experience?" but instead ask "What am I doing with attention right now?" Attention is always somewhere. We don't always notice where it is; often, it's on the world created by the thought of the moment. There isn't a "wrong" place to have attention. The point is to notice where it is, and what attention itself feels like, and how that differs from thinking.

Attention is *always* someplace. You can be deliberate about where you put it, or it can just wander, be easily distracted, caught up. When you were a little kid in school, and you'd drifted away from what the teacher was doing up there at the blackboard, and suddenly she clapped her hands and said *pay attention,* you were in fact already in rapt attention – just not on what she was doing. You were paying so much attention (to your daydream or to the kid making faces in the desk beside you) that you had no spare attention for the teacher's lesson on subtraction.

Attention is always doing something. But *seeing* what it's doing right now, and feeling what attention itself feels like, is another thing altogether. When you put attention on the fact that you're thinking, the thoughts themselves cease to entrance you, because you no longer mistake them for reality.

When your attention is given utterly to something you're doing or something within your field of awareness, your mind (have you noticed?) goes utterly quiet. There is no sense of being a somebody. All the stories are far away, unable to get your attention.

Joy in the Face of Suffering

How is it possible to live in this world, where suffering and deterioration are rampant, and yet be steadily at peace, even joyful? In the face of so much pain and decay, is it self-indulgent to be joyful?

You might bring these two things into one frame of awareness – the mess of the world (or your life) and the longed-for well-being inside – and if you allow them to touch one another, in your mind, you are likely to conclude that the one makes the other impossible. Or that the one makes the other unreasonable, as if a person doesn't somehow "deserve" joy, with all the suffering in the world. As if joy had to be earned.

There is no contradiction between the world's problems (or personal ones) and profound calm within. Always and everywhere, the answer is to just do what you are doing right now. Be where you are, in the immediate reality.

If you're lying in bed, and it's night and you're tired, the thing to do is sink into the arms of sleep. If you're at the site of a devastating natural disaster, and you hear a wrenching sob a few feet from where you stand, turn toward the sound. Go to that man who has just found his child's body crumpled beneath the wreckage. Rub his back. Listen to him weep and rage. Take his grief into your heart. Help him pick up his child's body.

If you are in your bed listening to the radio about this man and his child, take the two of them into your heart for a few moments, letting it hurt, as it must. Then turn off the radio and sleep.

It's possible to stand in unflinching recognition of the world's ongoing pain, to feel deep compassion, to take action that's within your reach, and also to sleep soundly. To live your days filled with well-being and ease. If joy requires circumstances to be a certain way, it will be endlessly elusive. If certain conditions are needed for light-heartedness to flower, then (since life is constantly in flux) inner peace will always be fleeting.

If joy comes to you from the outside, *it will be taken from you*. This is a law of nature immutable as gravity.

The only source of lasting well-being is within.

But where do we get it, you say? Oh, but it's already here. It's been here right along, the whole time you've been learning how to walk, sitting in desks and pews, having lovers, getting divorced, collecting achy body parts, getting promotions, losing your job, getting a diagnosis. The whole time you're watching the news and wringing your hands, pacing the waiting room, waiting in line, waiting for the phone to ring, waiting for the mail to come, waiting for an answer.

Waiting for your life to begin.

There is only one way to get to it, to find it. And that is to be only in the very moment you are in, only this – *whatever* it may hold. The content of the moment is completely irrelevant to This. Just *be* this moment. Don't think about it. Feel it. Let the past die. Let the future die. (They never lived anyhow, apart from in your head.)

Watch the news. See what's happening. Then turn it off. Don't carry it around with you. Either drive to the

airport and get on a plane and go there and do
something, or send money or make phone calls, if that
can help. Otherwise, eat your dinner. *Only eat your
dinner.* This exact succulent slice of zucchini, green
and seedy and soft. It is, right now, the only truth. It is
through the bite of zucchini that you get to the only
perfect joy that is to be had, ever.

When time has died for you, when your mind has
ceased its pointless turning of gears, you will not be
able to find your way out of this well-being. You will
not need a lover, nor beautiful clothing, nor a good
job, nor health, not recognition, nor hobbies. Nor
world peace, justice, wise leaders, revolution.
Nothing, nothing, nothing.

Imagine.

The Best Thing You Can Do for Yourself

It's the most radically relieving thing you can do for yourself. Radically illuminating. Simple. So simple a gesture, so uncomplicated. Unambiguous as a surgeon's knife.

Don't let it get complicated. Seize any impulse to *judge* and set it aside, far over there, with lots of space around it. Take any thought to *change* yourself and set it over there beside the temptation to judge. These two things must be far away, so far you forget they were ever an option.

Now come back here and look. Cleanly, with wide, inquisitive eyes, observe to what extent your experience of your life is determined by something going on in your head. Anything at all going on in your head.

You are thinking, *But it's unavoidable. Something will always be going on inside my head.*

Remember, the thought to change anything needs to be set aside.

Discover to what extent the way your life feels to you is shaped by mental activity, by the mind-made lens you look through.

You are thinking, *But it's important for the mind to process, to evaluate, to look out for danger, to hope for a better time.*

Relax the tendency to object. This isn't about second-guessing. It's about the willingness to notice. You're simply observing a phenomenon, as it's presently operating.

This isn't (above all) about improving your thoughts. It isn't about wresting control of your life by creating a spruced-up mental framework. It's about relaxing the wish to control.

It's about discovering, for yourself, the difference between a moment of real life and your mental handling of it.

We live inside our mental impressions of life.

You say, *But there's no choice about that.* Oh yes there is. You say, *But we are intelligent beings, and besides, the mind runs on automatic.*

It does, yes. And we have fine brains that are useful when they are useful.

This isn't about stopping thought. It's about seeing that thought is one thing and the direct, yielding encounter with reality is another.

The mind insists that it *has* to mediate. That to relax the habit of mediation would subject a person to danger.

Has your mind ever grown still? Have you been stunned to stillness? Have you had that experience where time has seemed to stop?

What did it feel like?

In the confrontation with a single riveting fact, has all the rest of the world – *and all thought* – fallen away?

In the physical presence of a beloved, the shock of devastating news, a sudden threat to your existence? A singer on a stage, her voice breaking your heart open and open and open? A labor contraction getting worse by the millisecond? A grenade you can see sailing toward you? Your body in purely focused effort (running at top speed, climbing a mountain)?

Where was the mind then? Where were *you?* Lost in the moment. Given utterly to the present thing. What strange calm suffuses a person at such a moment (even when it's a terrible moment).

But most moments aren't mind-stilling ones like these. Life is nearly all lived inside the head. So, we suffer.

This isn't about trying to change anything. The desire for things to be different, like the tendency to lament (or celebrate) what is seen, needs to be allowed to recede. These tendencies are structures that block the light. Just watch what happens inside the head. Observe the running background commentary, and see how it affects your feeling state.

Oh yes, it can all change. Not by your trying to make it change. But by the simple, clean gesture of watching what's actually going on, as you presently are. Trying to change yourself guarantees you never will. Try the other way, and see what happens.

What Life Is Actually Like

You have a picture of how you'd like life to be for this next stretch of the adventure. You make a plan to give shape to your days, to bring about the sort of thing you'd like to see happen. This is what a person does. As you take steps in that direction, the hope is that bits of delight and satisfaction – moments of actual life experience – will occur. (Otherwise, why bother?)

If you look, though, it's clear that even when the desired circumstances have come about, the vast majority of the moments in any given day are not those juicy nuggets of delight. Most of the moments a person lives are in fact boring, unremarkable, inconvenient, some kind of nuisance. Something to tolerate. You did not ask for those moments to be that way, and you would prefer that they hurry up and get over with so you can get on to the good stuff.

What you tell yourself about these kinds of moments is that they "don't count." They are what you have to endure to get to the fun parts. Even when what you've worked for is realized (and often, of course, it's not), most moments in a day, in a life, involve things having nothing to do with what you've identified as worthwhile. They are about sitting at a red light and being on hold and listening to somebody's rant and collecting records for your tax return and lying in bed sick.

Only, those throw-away times, the in-between times that don't seem to count, constitute virtually your entire life.

Isn't this worth looking at (sometime in advance of the death bed)?

Life is an ongoing conflict between how you'd like the moment to be and how it actually is. We don't let life be itself. It's constantly measured against a standard in the head. A huge amount of suffering occurs because of this ongoing disconnect between what's happening and what you'd rather be doing. We are simply not in charge of how a huge part of life unfolds. When you consider that just about your entire life is the moments that don't seem to count, is it any wonder there is so much pain?

Here's a question to ask yourself. What would life be like if that conflict weren't there? If you weren't constantly trying to bend life to your wishes, merely tolerating the boring or lousy 99%? What if you simply experienced what's happening, without resistance or mental management? How different would life feel?

No, really.

Imagine one of those inconvenient moments turning out to be one of your last. (This will, in fact, very likely be the case, though you may not realize this as it's occurring.) If someone said you had five minutes left, wouldn't those moments be delicious? This is the human problem, that life doesn't feel that way always.

When you look at how much effort you put into trying to shape your life, and then see how much of life is simply what comes down the pike, the stuff you have to merely abide, with you having no say in it whatever – well, isn't something wrong with this picture?

You keep thinking it's the moment's "content" that determines how it feels to you – that makes life feel the way it does. But what if it were the *awareness* in the moment that counted, the degree of presence that made the moment delicious or foul?

It's being in the now – really *being* – that brings about the experience of vitality and well-being that all the dreamed-of stuff is meant to generate. The exciting new partner, the better job, the improved body or clothing – it's all about wanting to enjoy life moment-to-moment. But simple presence is what gives juice to the moment, even one having boring or difficult content. Any moment you're awake to suffuses you with peace and vitality, whether or not what's happening is wonderful. When ordinary moments are fully experienced, it doesn't matter so much what's occurring, or whether the big-picture dreams are ever realized.

This is not just about surrendering to what-is. It's also about not chasing a certain kind of experience because you think it will Do It. It's about ceasing to wish you could mold life to your preferences, or expecting the satisfying status quo to hold.

This is not an argument against preferences or dreams. This is about learning what it feels like to pursue something you want but not have it completely deflate you if it doesn't materialize. It's about really being with whatever's happening, because attention itself generates delight. Attention to the present moment is how you can tell you're alive.

This is about living a satisfying, delightful life without ferocious attachment to everything you do. Whatever happens is okay. The 99% of your life that used to be something to get through, so you could get to the good parts – it ends up being juicy, for no good reason. And nothing's really changed. Except everything has changed.

What Am I?

The question is, What am I? What is the thing I don't want to have missed? What is life really about?

When someone has stopped suffering, when the mind has grown quiet, as the default, and is no longer generating angst, why is that? What has changed?

It's that you no longer feel – literally feel, in a bodied way – that you are all the things you thought you were. Your history, your opinions, your efforts, your fears and hopes. Your body, even. Some of these things still are in the picture: the body looks the same; the history did occur. But the opinions have grown thin to nil, and fear and hope no longer drive you. You've stopped identifying with the contents of your head, or your gut. Because all of that has stopped feeling like *you,* it loses juice, and pretty much ceases to function in that automatic way it always has.

If all of that doesn't feel like *you* anymore, what does? Awareness. Consciousness itself feels like the real you. Here it is: the visceral answer to *What am I?* The answer to the question doesn't come via the intellect. The ordinary mind has no access to this. It's a *felt* thing. On the order of this: you can *feel* when you're hungry, or tired, or awake as opposed to sleeping. The sensation of consciousness is like that.

(There is no perfect word for this. Here, "awareness" and "consciousness" are being used to suggest the same thing.)

When awareness is the primary reality, you don't experience that you're separate from your immediate surroundings, from the sensation or movement of your body. It's as though you *are* whatever you're aware of at the moment. Consciousness and whatever's "in" it are a unity. All you have of your "self," ever, is momentary experience. None of life is run through the familiar mental filters *(I like it, I don't like it, This is stupid, This is unfortunate)*. Nothing is resisted.

Awareness is the way you know something is happening. It isn't different from person to person. There's nothing personal to it. It doesn't change over the course of a life. Aware is aware. The way you can tell you're here, that you exist, is the same now as it was when you were five, and it will be the same just before you lose consciousness at the end. None of your life experience has altered awareness and it never will.

Consciousness is not affected by anything "in" it. It's the same, moment to moment, regardless of what's happening in it. It's like space.

If you wake in the night with your calf muscle starting to cramp, you are aware of the start of tightness and pain. The awareness watches the pain get worse, the tightness more so. The leg is changing, maybe the thoughts are intensifying *(God, I wish this would stop)*, but the awareness watching it all is its same self, moment to moment.

The fact that consciousness can notice the thoughts happening (and does not generate emotion) is vivid evidence that thinking and consciousness are not the same.

As the pain reaches its greatest intensity and gradually begins to unwind, the awareness is still there, watching, unchanged. When finally your calf is entirely soft and comfortable again, consciousness notices the absence of pain and tightness.

From start to finish, the consciousness has been its same self, unaffected by what's been happening in it.

What's happening in any moment – whether it's outer activity or physical pain or thinking or emotion – is just the momentary expression of a life. The content of life comes and it goes. This has been true of every shred of your life experience, and so it will continue. Change is constant, in the realm of content. None of it is "you." It's real, in a momentary kind of way. You're really there for it. It's just that you don't mistake it for *you*. The only continuity is the part of you that's aware of whatever's happening.

The reason you were born is to live life as *that*. As awareness.

Consciousness itself is where peace flourishes. It's where life is tingly and delicious, regardless of the particulars of what's happening *in* it. Strangely, maybe, it's *through* that very thing (the form life is taking at the moment) that consciousness experiences itself. Even when the particulars are what we may think of as difficult. Their unpleasantness or the challenge life presents is not the primary thing that impresses. What's front and center is that this is what *is*. What-is shimmers with life. Because the mind isn't dropping everything into categories, subjecting it all to the familiar assessments, awareness is left with encountering the plainness and the purity of reality.

From the point of view of the familiar self, this is incomprehensible. That self cannot encounter reality as it is, because the self is *made* of desire and opinion and self-image.

But if you watch what happens, in any moment of encountering anything at all (including something on your interior), you will see that unfiltered awareness occurs *prior* to judgment, prior to analysis and story-making. First, you see, you hear, you feel. *Then* the mental and emotional processing occurs. Awareness is the primary – the original – encounter with life.

Ask yourself what a moment of experience would be like – what it would *feel* like, how different it would be from the norm – if you lingered in plain awareness. If the next part didn't happen. If you didn't need to know what you thought about the thing. What it meant. If you didn't give it the power to put you in a certain kind of mood, or frame of mind.

The awareness is here all the time. It functions constantly. We can't *not* experience it. Awareness is the door to the world, to our lives. It's just that we don't usually pay attention to it. What gets our attention is all the stuff "in" awareness: what we're aware *of*. Which, more often than not, is the content of the inner narrative.

But as soon as your awareness shifts its focus from the story's content to the fact that thought is occurring, everything changes. Then, you know what you are.

What Happens at Awakening?

A question that gets asked (by others and also inside my own head) is this. Given that the sensation of sweet, unruffled well-being may occasionally visit a person, in which the mind is still and all apparent problems have dissolved, what is it that causes this condition to become the norm?

This is the compelling question. Mostly it gets asked because a person thinks that coming up with a possible answer may give rise to a possible method for getting there. The trouble with the idea of a method is that you're doing something *so that* you will "get somewhere" in the future, not for its own sake. You're doing it so that "you" will *change* . . . which is not what happens at awakening.

So you say – well, what's a person's incentive to (say) linger over the question *What am I?* What spawns that question? It comes of the longing to know the truth. It's an existential curiosity that's come alive. Which is very different from the desire to feel better, to stop suffering, to have mystical experiences.

Meanwhile, my own curiosity (without regard for a possible method) has led me to wonder and wonder. I watch someone tip over into the stable condition, or I encounter someone who's been that way for some time, and I'm curious about what might have happened to get them to the other side of that line – to that "place" where there is going to be no getting thrown off-balance, no becoming lost in thought, no identification or attachment, or mental or emotional anguish. Which is very different from the occasional fleeting taste of the sweet emptiness where nothing is experienced as wrong.

It seems that at some point the sense of self – of What You Are – stops having to do with the usual (personal history, beliefs, personality, desires, fears), and instead it has to do with spaciousness. Who You Are has more to do with present-moment awareness than with any sort of solid-seeming self that's apparently stable over time. You appear to be the space in which all is occurring (which is very different from the you that could bear a grudge or fear death).

Your dear old familiar self simply no longer feels like what you are. So, in the relieving absence of that burden, a whole new sense of reality takes over – including the reality of "you," the nature of life and time, the immediate scene, and other people. When that new sense of the real takes over, you cannot possibly be troubled, because "you" (in the familiar sense) are no longer operative.

At least, this is how it appears to me.

But then the question comes: okay, but what *causes* the old sense of self to finally completely dissolve? Maybe it's a matter of the made-up self being seen through enough times, so that it feels less and less real, until it ceases to hold together. Or maybe there's a shattering all-at-once blow to the self, such that its insubstantial nature is abruptly illumined. Maybe it's deep and sustained contemplation on the question *What AM I, anyway?*

There is no authoritative answer. I can't even say with confidence what happened in my own case.

At the very least (not to come too close to the primrose path of a possible method), it must surely be a good idea to keep an unwavering eye on the ongoing maintenance and expression of the dear old apparent self, the one that's able to suffer, to get lost in thought, to experience life as a series of problems and goals (among them, the search for a method to awaken). And to remember constantly that *this* self is not It. This self is incapable of sustained peace and well-being. All it does is block awareness of the deeper reality, where the enduring sweetness abides.

Whatever the longed-for *It* is, it isn't *that* old thing. See that much. And then, give it no more attention. For to give it attention – even to lament its apparent substance – is to encourage its ongoingness, its appearance of reality. Sort of like indulging a toddler who's having a tantrum. Or like pumping high-octane gas into the thirsty tank of selfhood.

Meanwhile, this other "you" is patiently waiting to take over, to gather you in its tender arms.

You Are Not Precious

It's said (and has been said for millennia) that it's possible for a person not to suffer, not to be subject to fear and desire. It's said that the essential nature of a human being is spaciousness, unconditional love without attachment or dissatisfaction. Those who know have said this condition is inherent to all people, however unrealized it may be, however unaware of this nature they may be, however disguised and buried it is beneath all that occupies their awareness all their lives, until the heart lets out its last beat.

Most people hearing this idea discount it. A few sit down with it, some in a devoted way, some of them for decades. Seldom is the longed-for condition realized. Seldom does even the most devoted seeker after truth come to live in it, throughout each ordinary day, to experience life's ups and downs in equanimity that is without strain, or vigilance, or effort.

Why is this? Why, if it is our very nature, do we not live there? Why does what becomes so obvious to one – vivid as the colors of maples in the fall – remain hidden to the greater part of humankind, even to those who long for it?

Some version of this question has been occupying me for a long time. This must be the difference between the person who retreats into anonymity and the one who remains engaged in the human world. One has given up trying to answer the question, or maybe always knew better than to try, and the other hasn't given up, for the sake of the ones longing to know what they really are.

* * * * *

You are not precious, I want to say. And then: Notice
what that statement does to you. What edge it sets
your teeth on. What offense may be taken. The
possible shock to the system.

The one who wants to feel good about himself,
herself . . . who wants to heal, to *matter* somehow . . .
the one who has suffered . . . is not precious. But
seems to be. The one with armfuls of stories,
triumphs, regrets. The one that is misunderstood, to
whom being understood, or valued, matters so much.
The one capable of being wounded, or uplifted by
praise. What if this self turned out to be superficial?
One enormous distraction from the deeper something
you are.

All the beliefs that have collected – about what's true,
important, inevitable. The elaborate structure that has
built itself around all your days, something to carry
you along, to make life somehow – barely –
manageable. What if it all ceased to feel precious, to
require upkeep, improvement?

The self that matters so much has no access whatever
to the underlying reality. The self makes no contact
with the essence. It is not transformed into it. The two
have nothing to do with one another.

The self that appears to be precious functions in only
one regard to the "Self" that is, in fact, unfathomably
precious: *it obscures it*. This – the apparent value of
the ordinary self – is why the deeper truth is so rarely
assumed as one's day-to-day reality.

Like an exquisite garment put on, the essence of a
human being is simple, plain, remarkable in its
lightness. How many times in an ordinary day are you
brought to a rush of gratitude – just for *this*, this that

runs in your veins, that is here no matter what – that has nothing whatever to do with who you once thought yourself to be?

What could be more precious? Worth the cost of everything? And what is that *everything?* What has lost its former dear value? The heart that ached, that took offense, needed mending. The self that wanted, that mattered.

It's the very self that believed if it meditated enough, or cultivated the right behavior or attitude, it would somehow become free of its self-made burdens. Would transform itself into what which never was burdened in the first place.

It isn't how it works.

What happens, when it happens, is that you cease investing in the woundable self as being real. It stops seeming like what you *are.* It stops mattering.

Why is it that when this miracle occurs, a person will inevitably say – *I feel as if I've come home? It's been here all along, I now see, waiting for me.* It is recognized, felt to be familiar. Why is that?

Because it – what you *really* are – has been with you from the beginning. Alongside the self that once appeared so precious, so truly what you believed yourself to be. You might have had glimpses of the perfect stillness, where time and dissatisfaction do not exist. Maybe in childhood, or since then, in some kind of extremity. Some moment of stunning beauty, in which "you" did not seem to be there, or didn't seem to be separate from the beauty. Your problems disappeared, briefly. Lost all substance. They left with *you.*

Yet something, some dazzling awareness, sensed its own reality. Then, shortly after, was eclipsed. For the rest of life, perhaps.

It could be otherwise.

The Day Time Dies

First light. It's like the first time Adam and Eve opened their eyes and saw green, and one another. That's what it's like. Here you are, fifty years old (or 72 or 21), already lived a good bit, with things a certain way. In my case, five decades of it, all the assumptions of all those years. By fifty you've learned a lot – what to assume is possible, and mostly, what's not possible. That's what we call maturity. Being well balanced, in the way of psychology, personality, societal norms. Not to expect too much in the way of ease or joy. Just get along. Find your pleasure and relief and meaning where you can.

And then, like somebody just lifted the shade on a morning like this one, you are utterly innocent. All the clothing is gone. The costumes that have kept you safe, or being somebody. You can't remember why you used to think you had problems. That you couldn't cope, or had to sort something out, or make something happen.

You look in the mirror, because you half expect to look entirely different, physically speaking. Because nothing whatever is recognizable in the feeling state. Your mind is as still as a pond on a windless day.

The image in the mirror, to your quiet surprise, is familiar. Well, except the heaviness around the eyes and mouth is missing.

The feeling is that the most extraordinary thing that could ever happen to anyone has happened to you. And not because you deserved it, or caused it. The combination of these two things – the apparent randomness of the blessing and the fact that this is the ultimate condition of a human being – has the feel of miracle.

You are Adam, you are Eve. You are the green. You are the light filling up your eyes, your belly. The irrepressible smile will not undo itself.

Whatever else is going on, in an outer kind of way, *this* is always the main thing in your awareness. Nothing eclipses it. There is no forgetting. You *are* the remembering.

Everything else is laughable. All the ways you felt sorry for yourself. Tried to fix yourself, or somebody else. It all looks poignant. How scary death looked. How much safety seemed to matter.

Time has erased itself. Thought got shocked into crumbling. Look at the green! How it makes itself all over again. How there isn't anything but light.

You notice, as regular life stuff keeps happening, that there's no assumption of anything continuing as it is. This isn't consciously thought, let alone said to self, but it's the case. You can tell because of the absence of surprise, when there's a change in something. When something stops, or changes direction, or disappears, or suddenly occurs.

The absence of assumption, of wishing for stability, predictability, means that there's no struggle to accept. It also means that there's a constant savoring, a really *being with* the moment and its blessing. Because something in you, in a background sort of way, is aware that this may be the final time, or the only one, that you'll be with this person, or in this place, or doing this thing, or feeling this way. So you pay attention. You're really with it. You *are* it, the thing that's happening. You let love come up into your bones like warm water.

There's a recognition, as the thing is occurring. You pat the dog goodbye, so she understands you're about to leave, in her old-and-deaf dog stupor by the wood stove. Something in you knows you may not be back, even though you're just going grocery shopping. That same something in you knows her heart may beat its last while you're out. You aren't consciously thinking these things, as you stroke her black head and murmur close to her ear about how she's going to stay. It's just that there's no assumption of how anything will be later. *Later* beginning when you turn away from the dog and move through the door.

Later doesn't compute. Living doesn't happen later. It happens now. Nothing vital is making assumptions. The mind is not where vitality is felt. The mind is the assumer, the future-looker, the seeker after patterns, the wisher for security, reliability.

The mind is still.

So, the smell and feel of the dog, and the look in her brown eyes, as they register your imminent departure. This is all there is.

It is constantly this way. You don't miss anything. You're really there for it. It may never happen again. Patterns no longer are discerned. Unforeseen balls *will* come sailing in out of left field. You know it has always been this way, and that much won't change.

The sudden balls don't startle. You hadn't been assuming otherwise. There is the constant readiness to yield, to bend. The absence of the tension of grasping and hoping and dreading means receptivity is exquisite. Recognition is unbounded. Almost unbearable in its sweetness.

The machinery that kept going a self has broken. What broke? What has ceased to function?

The power supply of a self is belief. It's the belief that what appears to be real actually is. That the mind's impression is a reliable indicator of reality.

So, for instance, time appears to be real, to have an existence outside the thinking mind. You *think* it into being, but you believe it's real – out there. That time goes on independent of your looking before and after.

But then, on a day that will later mark the beginning of your life, something occurs that causes you to see the qualitative difference between present-moment existence and memory, or an image of a possible future development. One – the past or future item – occurs in your mind. The other – the present – occurs in your viscera. One is felt, lived. *Before* understanding, before story or label. It is attention, encounter, movement, sensation. It has to do with an intelligent physical aware body located in space. It has to do with the smell of a dog's head. The other occurs at a remove from any of this. It comes into being, as it were, in the mind.

You have never once actually lived in the actual past or the future, nor ever could. But only in a stream of thoughts about something before or after now.

The day this deeply dawns, not just as a thought but the way a shock of electricity penetrates your body – that day that time is allowed to stop, or more truly, to be seen as the mental invention it only ever was – you will see as the day you finally came utterly alive. No longer capable of regret, or wistfulness, or fear.

If there is only, really, the now, if the products of the mind are secondary to momentary reality, how can there be a self? To visualize a self, you need to open the door to the mind and revisit your history, your ideas about things, your identity. You need, in short, to remember.

Who is somebody that has no ability to retrieve memory? Those around that person will say it's as if that one has already died. The familiar person isn't there. But from the point of view of the person who is only the now, *someone* is in fact there, if only enough to realize no memory is retrievable. It's just that there's no continuity. No identity.

But something ("somebody") is there, aware. Even if only enough to be disoriented. Belligerent, maybe. Afraid.

It's not that we're "better off" without memory, without the capacity to envision a future. It's about what happens to the sense of self, of reality, when you viscerally get the difference between any of the mind's content and the sensation of aliveness that attends, only and ever, the now.

Do You Love Yourself?

If you don't love yourself (which many people say they do not), the answer is not to learn how to love yourself. All the self-help books, and plenty of psychotherapists, want you to think you need to love yourself — that you "cannot love someone else" unless you "love yourself" first.

[Before you read on, pause to notice: how is this sitting in your awareness, *right now?* This idea that the goal of self-love is somehow off the mark. What is your mind doing with this idea? What degree of dissonance has (perhaps) been stirred?

Now, without trying to settle the dissonance; without trying to "figure out" anything you've read so far; without trying to resolve anything . . . simply set aside whatever just happened in your head, and keep reading.]

When you are free, when you have awakened, you neither love nor hate yourself. You neither accept nor reject yourself. You neither forgive nor blame yourself. You just are what you are, moment to moment, as "what you are" shows up in actual life. It doesn't occur to you to love yourself or not love yourself. You *are* love.

The question of how you feel about yourself has gone away. Including the matter of there even being a "you," a solid, sustained thing that moves through time. A self that can be affected, that can have feelings or thoughts about itself.

The problem (notwithstanding all the hard work of therapists and self-help books and well-meaning friends to convince us otherwise) is *not* the inability to love yourself. The problem is prior to that. It's that you seem substantial to yourself. You seem real, separate. Lovable or not-lovable. You are aware of your *self* in a way that is excruciating. In awakeness, though, you have lost interest in yourself.

Imagine that: finding yourself no longer of interest.

I used to find myself endlessly interesting. I was my favorite subject. The memoir, as a form, was *invented* for the likes of me. Well, this is mostly true of people – not the memoir part maybe (not everyone is a writer), but the self as center of the moving universe. Everywhere I went, I stayed the center of things. The universe (as my head created and projected it) went with me.

This is how it is with a person. Everywhere you ever go, the center of the universe has just moved to where you now are. Where you are now, in this moment – *that* is the molten core of your planet, around which your satellite moons careen, the people and issues whose orbits are familiar, held to you by terrific gravitational force. Moving as you move. Always, at the center is *you*.

Some of myself I liked, or maybe loved, but most of me I did not love. Most of me I wanted to improve, or conceal, or ditch altogether. I wanted help with me. I wanted more of a lot of things: more love, more success, more security, more money. I wanted more recognition, admiration. Not (as I guiltily supposed was the case) because I needed bolstering, because my "self-esteem" was low. But – the actual truth – *because I thought I was real*. Substantial. I thought the idea of me in my head (that molten core center of all) was a real thing. That a *me* existed that was independent of the idea in my head. I thought that the person I saw in the mirror was identical to the ideas I had of myself. The ideas of *who I am,* including things like *do I love myself.* Things like the collection of historical data (my beloved story, food for memoir). The beliefs. The roles. The traits, including the traits I wanted other people to know me by. *Love me for.*

I thought all those things about myself were independently real. And certainly important! (The person they constituted was, after all, the center of the universe.)

Everybody is the center of a universe: their own. When they move, the center of their universe moves. An endless sea of universes. The universes collide with one another all the time, each telling the other indignantly that it ought to pay more attention to what it's doing. What that really means is, how dare you think you are the center of the universe, when of course it's clear that *I* am that.

It's a wonder we can stand to be near one another at all. Never mind have relationships that aren't brimming with conflict.

Never mind wake up . . . *from the whole thing.*

When you stop trying to fix what can never be anything but broken (the person who is the subject of the self-help books); when you stop demanding love, stop demanding attention, and you just *be* it – *be* love, *be* attention – then the feeling of bottomless need goes away.

You aren't the center, anymore, of your universe. You can't bump into any other universes either, because you aren't at a distance from any of them. You *are*

them, and they are you. The question of whether you
love yourself has gone away. The need to be loved –
even by yourself – has dissolved into the sky.

No More Big Sighs: The End of the Search for Security

Sometimes a person will seek to awaken because of a hunger for an all-encompassing solution to life's difficulties. A kind of global guarantee of okayness. Freedom can be seen as a source of security.

What is security? In ordinary life, it's establishing circumstances expected to provide stability and safety. A reliable set-up of some kind, a stable sort of container for life to move along in. The desire for security often comes of having not had it, or being afraid of losing it. Something to do with physical circumstances, financial well-being, health. Knowing you will have ready access to what you need. That you won't have to reinvent the wheel, or maybe do without, every time a need arises. When the rain is falling, there will be a roof to get under. When there are meds to buy, there will be money, or a health plan, so you can get them. A reliable car in the driveway, or proximity to good public transportation. Somebody to look out for you when you need help or love.

Sometimes when some of this hasn't come together very well, a person will turn to the spiritual life as an alternative source of security and well-being. A set of beliefs enabling faith, a way to believe that all will be well, that the universe is benign, that a divine goodness is overseeing all. There's a wish for life to be understandable. Life is seen as a series of lessons, or the playing out of karma or destiny, something with a larger meaning. A frame of reference to make the hard times tolerable or at least comprehensible.

Something. Anything.

When a person awakens, no assurance of security comes with the revelation of the truth. What happens is that you've stopped needing any sort of promise that all will be well. It stops mattering. You stop looking for meaning. It stops being important to be able to count on something, somebody. Yourself even.

When you wake up, you stop caring very much about what happens to you. Not because you don't cherish your life. No, it's that you no longer feel quite real to yourself, at least not in the way you used to. Why would you need to keep yourself in a certain kind of condition when you have nothing to lose? You have let go completely of needing to keep your sense of self intact. You cannot be threatened. You're okay with whatever happens.

How can you feel afraid of something unknown, something in the future, if only *this moment* feels real to you?

What you come to see is that there never *was* any security. Ever. Only the impression of it. That is the truth, and one of the things about awakeness is that it is entirely comfortable with changeable reality. It's no longer uncomfortable in the presence of even an ugly or painful truth. The truth is, even when you thought you had attained some kind of security, in your life before, you hadn't really. Secretly, you knew this. (We do know this.) It's just that – well, back then, when security was something you valued, you sort of held your breath, day to day, year after year, hoping the flimsy edifice would remain roughly stable. During the intervals when it did hold (by luck mostly), you told yourself (because you wanted to believe it) that now you had things pretty much together, and maybe this time it would be for keeps.

The problem is, you always deeply knew that someday something would go wrong. For instance, you always knew death would come. (The trend is observable.) The fact that we can manage to forget death is coming, most of the moments we live, is the ultimate indicator of the thinness of the appearance of safety.

So when somebody wants to find their way to a reliable, solid piece of ground to stand on, and they think waking up will provide that, I want to look them in the eye and gently say – well, no, it doesn't work like that.

You don't wake up so you can finally feel safe. You wake up because you want to stop needing safety and predictability. You wake up because you want to know what it's like to live in the present instead of in the future.

For what can security possibly mean, if there is never any such thing as tomorrow? as continuance? as predictability? If this moment, this exact one right here, really is the only one that's ever real (this is one of the pieces of truth that smacks you right in the face, when you wake up), then how can the question of providing for the future even be taken very seriously? And if you don't have any built-in resistance mechanism, whatever any moment holds is just what it is – neither okay nor not-okay. Just *real*.

Oh, of course you will keep paying the rent and registering your car and putting gas in it and trying to save a little money. The practical stuff will keep happening, as it should. But you will stop being in the least invested in any of it holding up as it might have previously. You won't assume anything will continue, let alone improve.

When you are awake, none of the little successes gives you a warm fuzzy feeling anymore. Nor does some upheaval in your life turn your stomach to water or interfere with your sleep. You pretty much stop having big sighs of despair and big sighs of relief. You no longer identify with how things are going in your life. None of it affects your sense of self worth, well-being, security. The ever-changing circumstances are a practical matter, that's all. You respond as you need to, and you move on.

So if you appear to have the circumstances that amount to somebody's idea of security, you don't feel any different inside from how you'd feel the day after some or all of it fell completely apart.

Because it isn't about you. It just isn't. And you know what? It never *was*. You just thought it was.

Life on the Tongue

Freedom is living unencumbered. You are free to move easily among whatever things come along. You are soft, without the tension of doing, of anticipation; without the readiness to defend. Yet by some miracle, whatever comes toward you, however hard, from whatever direction, however abruptly, the body yields just the right amount. Balance is not interfered with.

There is no rigidity, no expectation, no fear. No resistance. Playing in the background of awareness, like a song, there is the steady but relaxed knowing that anything could happen at any moment. The prospect of this is not in the least troubling. Contentment is the same, whether you remain at rest or whether something comes at you, stirring you to fluid response. You are unchanged, deeply, by what happens.

You want nothing. Why is this, after a lifetime of ravenous need? You still enjoy; you know what you prefer. But it's all extra delight, that's all. Why is this? If you look, you will see: you want nothing, in the old way, because – after years and decades of striving, longing, needing – you have realized you *are* everything. How could you possibly want? How could dissatisfaction get a toehold?

The self that needed things to be a certain way, that sought security and reassurance and meaning, no longer feels real to you. The familiar you seems like a two-dimensional drawing of life, of a person. You see how it was all the scribbling of the mind, scratching in the dark to establish a sense of importance. Trying to hold terror at bay – the dread of meaninglessness, of insufficiency. Helplessness.

How can it be that it's all stopped mattering? Where did fear go? But when you look, you see: it isn't that fear left, exactly, leaving you your same self, sans fear. No, it's that the self capable of fear (and desire and shame and all the rest of it) came to be insubstantial. Like a mesh mantle in a lantern that holds its shape after you've burned it the first time, sufficient to hold flame many times after. But if, between episodes of burning, you touch the mantle, it dissolves into powder on your fingertip. It never *was* the solid thing it appeared to be.

We are like that. The sense of what a person is is just like that: powder.

What turns out to be real, the only substance you can hold on your tongue and get the sweet of, is the encounter with *this moment.* The sweet of it or the acrid, it's the same. Alive aware sensate intelligence with life on the tongue, just now. That's it. Ever and always. That's what you *are;* that's what you have. Period. Then the next thing comes along, and you're there for it. You *are* it. Everything else is in the head. Memory, belief, story, grudge, hope.

When freedom takes you over, everything in the head has turned to powder and drifted away on the breeze. And you? You are really here. Finally! You're perfectly still inside but are outwardly in motion, the expression of "you" changing moment to moment. Because *life* is that way. It always was like this. Only now, you know it.

The Endless List of Things to Do

How does it feel to have an endless list? What is it to have too much to do in a given space of time, to live in thrall to a sense of duty? And . . . how does it feel when you finish everything, and then could theoretically finally rest, but seem too restless to do so? You want to get through the list so you can finally take it easy. But if that blessed moment ever comes – if the unencumbered afternoon at last arrives, or the long-anticipated week of vacation – you find yourself antsy, bored, unable to really and truly let down. What is all of this about?

What if when you were doing something, you weren't mentally urging toward the thing you'll do when that's finished, whether it's the next thing on the list or the chance to sit down and breathe? What if you really *did* the thing you're doing and had all of your attention there? Even if the thing you're doing is cleaning the toilet or changing the oil in your car. What if it weren't a thing to be crossed off a list, but instead occupied all of your attention? How different life would feel. The list would no longer be a cinderblock hanging from a rope around your neck. And you wouldn't be so constantly desperate to have a break (and then unable to really enjoy it when it comes).

You're going to do the thing one way or the other. Why not be present with it, instead of hurrying ahead in your mind to what you'll do next?

What we actually want is not "nothing to do." The thing we crave is the easing of the pressure that drives the list-fulfillment, the terrible pressure we constantly put ourselves under. When you do just the one thing

you're doing, without allowing into the picture the
pressure of all that remains to be done, then you're at
ease doing that one thing. There's no stress to desire
relief from. The stress isn't (as it appears) because
there's a list of things to do. It's there because the
mind is constantly reviewing all that's ahead, looking
at each thing as if it were actually occurring now. You
can visualize its happening, can picture yourself doing
it, getting it done. The satisfaction of it, the relief of
having it accomplished, maybe even the delight. As if
you could somehow do all of that stuff in advance, by
thinking about it. As if multiple futures, in which all
these things were being accomplished, can co-exist.
You convince yourself you're capable of getting more
done than you actually are, so you're in a constant
state of frustration because you never get it all done,
and so (you tell yourself) you cannot enjoy and focus
on the one thing you're doing.

The mind confuses a mental picture of anticipated
activity with actual real life. You can't do a thing
ahead of time; what anticipating does is cause stress
that could have been avoided. Nothing real gets
accomplished.

We end up with too much to do because our ability to
live things ahead of time gives us the impression that
we're able to accomplish more, in a given stretch of
life, than we actually are. Because the mind is such an
able convincer of the present-moment reality of an
envisioned scene, something in us registers that it's
possible to fit into a certain stretch of life – an
afternoon, an hour, a vacation – more things than it
will actually, in present-tense reality, accommodate.
We keep being brought up short by the misalignment
between all there is to do and how much time there is
to do it in. We do not have a good time doing any of it,

and what satisfaction accrues from getting things done is very thin soup.

It appears, therefore, as if multitasking were possible, even necessary. What multitasking yields is multiple things halfheartedly done, and a body in constant stress. The present moment is not experienced because of the never-ending urging toward the next thing.

Then death comes.

When the mental list is carried around (that cinderblock), there is the ongoing sense of not having enough time, never getting to it all, alongside the felt *necessity* to get it done. The result is that we often are not really doing the one thing that is actually occurring at the time (which would put us in the present), because the mind is simultaneously "doing" one or two or twelve other things. It is this terrible pressure that we crave rest from.

No wonder.

If a person can really and truly do this one thing here, without letting the mind horn in with what's next, or what's being neglected, then there will be pleasure, or at least peace, in the momentary doing. There won't be such a need for rest, because the pressure won't be there. Also, the list will inevitably shorten itself, as the sense of what's truly doable in a given period of time will come more nearly in line with what you aspire to.

When you're present with the thing you're doing, you don't long to be done. You're just doing what you're doing, feeling alive. Present.

Anger as a Pointer

Anger – whether outwardly expressed or concealed – is a response to something underlying it, something felt *before*. A bite. Panic. A punch in the gut. Anger is what occurs *after*. Often that prior feeling was hurt, damage, fear. To focus on the anger, as if it's the "problem," is to linger on the surface of things. Trying to deal with anger itself might help a person cope, or behave better. It will not bring about freedom.

Sometimes anger turns in on itself, morphing into depression, putting the "real" problem even further out of reach. The numbness becomes its own paralyzing fog.

Sometimes the recognition of the power of anger will lead a person toward spiritual practice, supposing this might be the route to managing it, or perhaps "healing" it. But the idea of healing anger is like a cat licking a surface wound: the skin may knit, but the pus is trapped below the surface, making infection inevitable.

Anger is a symptom. Let it be a light directing attention toward the deeper vulnerability, the thing that gave rise to it in the first place. Like everything the ego does for us, anger is meant to be protective. Look at the thing it means to protect, at the point of origin, where vulnerability lives.

When fear is the underlying thing, if you're willing to see what's really there, there will likely be something about the absence of control, the inability to predict the future. Better by far to let yourself know these truths – to rest in the truth of the unknowable – than to live in the poison of the anger that means to protect you from that unwelcome truth.

The way to deal with anger is not to cultivate a mask of civility. It's not to escape into mystical experiences or bodies of belief. To become free, it's necessary to move *toward* the anger, the defensiveness, the righteous indignation – to see what's *beneath* it – and then to feel that profoundly vulnerable sensation, *in the body*. Without making reference to what the mind has to say about any of it.

The story must go. Or if it persists in telling itself, you must recognize that this is happening, and see the purpose of the story: to protect you from the pain that gave rise to it in the first place.

Maybe it's the thing you didn't get (your mother or father's love; safety; a good life with a partner). Maybe it's the terrible thing you experienced, perhaps at the hands of someone who meant you harm. It could be something going on right now. Or a string of financial or professional or relationship disasters. Something to do with your physical well-being.

So you got mad at life. You developed a story about how you'd been wronged, neglected, abandoned. About how life has had it in for you. You began to define yourself as a survivor. A loser. Somebody told you anger was healthy. You believed them.

You can tell yourself forever that you're "entitled" to your anger. If you keep believing that, you will die angry. If you're bound and determined to cling to this identity, give up the spiritual life. Save yourself a lot of trouble, and illusion.

You don't have to know the origin of the pain, in a mental, psychoanalytic way. What's important is that you *feel* it, in the body. That you see anger as an indication of an underlying wound, and that you see the story you've made out of it, and what refuge you take in that story.

The spiritual life, for some, amounts to the forging of a spiritual identity. Adopting a spiritual practice (identity, beliefs) has become, in recent times, the frontier beyond other modes of attempting to deal with unresolved pain. As if it's all on the same spectrum of "ways to deal with life." There was therapy and medication, and the consolation of numbing substances, and there were various New Age remedies, and then . . . now . . . there is the pursuit of spiritual awakening, or at least the prospect of exciting spiritual experiences having to do with being out of the body or something apparently psychic. At the very least, coping better, via meditation or some other method.

After years, maybe, of depression or self-loathing (as if you "deserved" what happened to you), it can look like it's healthy to get in touch with the anger, to express it. Like it's progress to become angry, if all you've done so far is beat yourself up, having believed all the negative messages you were given about yourself. Anger can be exhilarating for a while. Life-affirming, as it may appear. The forging of an identity out of a painful history can seem to be a kind of triumph over adversity.

See what it's like to allow yourself to sit in the bodied sensation of the terrible sorrow, the gripping fear, the absence of what you wish you had, or the pain of the thing you wish had never happened. *Sit in reality*. The feeling of the hurt itself. If the absence of cherishing or safety or success of some kind is deep in you, allow yourself to rest there. Without ideas about it. Just the physical sensation of it. Lay your head down and let it take you in its arms.

It's there anyhow. It's been there right along. You might as well make your peace with it. It doesn't have to define you forever.

It won't kill you. It might even free you.

Meanwhile, if you *don't* rest in it, you will continue to be imprisoned in anger. And wondering why you're never at peace.

Also, see (for pity's sake, *see)* how you have carved from your pain an identity. See how you'll be damned if you'll give that up. How entitled you feel you are to your story. How it's become a way of relating to people in your life.

If this "makes you mad," a light should be going on. (But you'll look where it points only if you want to become free of the whole mess.)

You think you want to be free? You may be kidding yourself. If it's freedom you want, really and truly – if you want to know what you are that's beyond the reach of anger, of any story at all – you need to be willing to let your heart break. If you've allowed your painful background or your present-tense life to define you, the brave thing is to see that truth. To ask: *Am I willing to be done with that identification?*

Retreats are sometimes attended by people who carry themselves in a certain way, straining to appear and behave as if they are at peace inside. Anger is often just below the surface. But the concealed anger isn't what's important: it's the thing *beneath* it that comes across most vividly, that tender, broken thing in their eyes – the pain they cannot bear to rest in.

But people don't want to go there. The whole point of retreats (they think) is to *escape* the pain. To distance themselves from it. They take on a spiritual identity whose purpose is to mask the deeper identity, the wounded something that never got over itself *and doesn't actually want to*. Because to set it down would be to leave behind what feels like their very self.

Oh, the irony: the way past the identity is to turn *toward* it, to see how it comforts and defines (and limits) you.

Every once in a while somebody sees through all of this in themselves. Or simply collapses, weary, into the agony. They sink into the pit and sob. Then they come back up for air, clean and fresh, relieved, the identity put down. Seen for the burden it always was. The thing is, it can't be let go until it is fully and consciously assumed. Felt. Seen for what it is, the light shining right through it. You see what the identity has done for you – and *to* you. The burden of it! The very thing it seemed would rescue you – the story about the awful thing – became a leaden thing you've hauled around.

It might have served its purpose for a time, but without it, you can freely move. You can feel the air move over every surface of your skin.

All That's Happening

What a surprise it's turned out to be, a repeating revelation, that the ordinary and the miraculous are the same. The most unremarkable episode, a sliver of plain-old life, in which nothing worthy of note appears to be taking place – how can it be that *this* is the occasion, again and again, for the feeling of blessedness?

The recognition is felt in the body, almost electric. It's as if an angel just appeared, saying *Behold*. I behold. I am beholden. I am held. I can hardly believe it. *This again.*

And all that's happening is that the floor is horizontal and smooth, and my feet move over it. All that's happening is that the blanket pulled up around my shoulders is soft, and contains my heat. All that's happening is the people on the radio are murmuring in the dark, telling stories about other people.

Each shift of awareness is like the click of a camera: behold, rejoice, be saturated.

Why would I ask life to be any certain way? How could dissatisfaction possibly enter the scene? How could I need something to do?

Look: the pillows on the couch, three dimensions, texture, color, noise, movement. As if I never saw or heard or felt any of it before now. Reflection, distance, direction. Something unseen but felt. Succession. Upside down, right-side up. Geometry. Angles. Transparency.

Visitor from another planet, is how it feels. Only, it's all the stuff I see every day. It's like being a child, discovering the world for the first time. Over and over again. Nothing routine, unnoticed, taken for granted. Always, the angel.

One night recently, I said to the dark of my still room, where I sat up in bed, *Why did this come to me, oh Lord? Why this blessing?* I could never tire of saying thank you. *Who are you, that I thank?* I said then. *How are you possibly knowable?*

Maybe death happens because we cannot stand anymore not to know. Splintered off from the beloved all our earthly existence, like satellites, we are gathered back into that which has whispered to us all our lives. We were handed the voices of crickets, promises that one day we would have the whole thing back. That we would be inside the heart of the cricket, the cricket turning out to be inside the body of the beloved, one thing nested inside the other, inside the other, all the way to everything.

Just Here

There is a simple, transformative thing a person can do to bring calm into the picture in a moment of stress. When you become aware of being caught up in anger or fear or frustration, take a moment to breathe, to feel yourself be. Say to yourself, *I'm just here.*

What does that mean, just here? It means alive, aware, in *this* place, *this* moment. Not in some other time or place, which the mind has probably been insisting was possible (even necessary). There's often a discrepancy between where you are and where your attention is. You're here, but your thoughts and emotions are focused on something happening later today, or happening now but elsewhere, or something that occurred earlier in the week, or twenty years ago. The result of the split between body and mind is often an ill-at-ease feeling, or worse, real emotional turmoil – and about something that's only "real," just now, inside your head.

The recipe for peace, always, is to have attention on present-moment reality, without resistance.

Just here, remind yourself. This is the only place you are, or can be. When you whisper that to your mind, its contents may lose color and momentum, restoring you to a little calm and presence, where you can simply feel yourself *be.* In present-moment awareness, your heart slows down. The tension unwinds. You can feel your breathing. Your here-ness. Ah . . . Things are more okay than you realized.

Almost always, here – this moment – is pretty much okay, especially if you aren't tightened against whatever's happening in the present. When you're able to see that the source of the pain isn't what's around you this moment, but is a string of thoughts that your mind has convinced you are real, the tension will have a chance to relax. Deeply taking in *just here* is like being gently led into a warm, still pool in the middle of the ruckus.

Just here, just here.

It means something else too, something deeper. *Just here* means simply being. Not doing something or being somebody. For the moment, simply here. Aware. Still. Existentially *here*. Your awareness is the space in which the present moment is happening. You can sense this. It's the experience of pure *I am* (the thing Nisargadatta talks about). Not (just for these few restful moments) I am *a parent*, or I am *bewildered,* or I am *trying to improve things in my life*. The end of any possible sentence has dropped off, leaving you with the unencumbered experience of *I am*. Feel the essence that remains. Feel how peaceful it is.

Just here. Here for the moment. That's enough. You don't need to have an opinion just now, to do something. You're just here.

Something in each of us – something fundamental, the stuff we're made of – is plain, unresisting awareness. Something in us is capable of being just here. Perfectly still and empty. Nothing more to it. At your center is a profound and quiet neutrality. An alert, radically allowing presence. When you grow quiet enough to sense this, in a moment of busy or challenging life, there is no place for torment to take hold.

Something in you is just here. *Really* here. And not anyplace else.

It's Not About Liking It

Get to the inside of what it feels like when resistance comes, or acceptance, and what is the difference in the quality of each, how one feels different from the other. Learn about this: how the point of non-resistance isn't about whether you are *glad* a thing happened, or whether you would prefer it were otherwise.

It *seems* that way – that acceptance is inherently related to agreeing-with, and resistance is somehow justified if a thing is deemed bad. But those connections are the very sources of the pain a person feels. They are the problem.

And it isn't about being a doormat, or about not trying to bring about change. It's about allowing the *fact* of a thing, and then maybe you go from there to say: *Okay, what's next? What could I do from* **here**? When "here" is the peaceful state that has come from acceptance of a thing, whatever comes next is likely to go better – to be informed with greater clarity, to be more peaceful-feeling and so take less of a toll. The result is that any action taken to improve things is more likely to have the desired outcome. (And you aren't compounding your own suffering by being negative about an already negative thing.)

But if the starting place is (instead of acceptance) a tight refusal to allow the fact of a thing – the fact that some unwelcome development is indeed the case, for the moment anyhow – then there is recklessness and misdirected energy, and costs along the way. When resistance flares, when anger and frustration and judgment are the fuel of some corrective action, often as much harm is done as good.

Acceptance can profitably be brought to an event that has taken place in one's immediate life circumstances or in the larger world, or it can be brought to some internal thing – a body sensation or an emotion or a thought. A mood. A state of mind. It is all the same; the experience of allowing, of not contracting against it, is the same, regardless of what is being allowed, and regardless of where the thing is located (present, past, body, mind, environment). *Allowed* doesn't mean agreed with. It means *seen*, without rushing to oppose, judge, deny, tell a story about.

A flood of peacefulness comes when resistance is seen and allowed to let go of itself. The eyes rolling up in the skull, the tsk-tsk-tsk, the muttering, the name-calling. *Damn-I-should-have-known, been-more-careful. She shouldn't do that. Oh no! it can't be! What now? What a mess.*

Approaching the light and it turns yellow, speeding up to get through it and – uh-oh, there's a cop, hard on the brakes. *Soft.* Go soft now. It's possible to stop hard and be soft inside. Not to say *damn* or *whew, that was lucky.* Didn't make it through the light: just a fact. No need to go to *Now I'm gonna be late.* Skip it. (Maybe it's true; but cursing about it won't make it un-true.) A flood of peacefulness, simply by accepting what is.

It isn't just about trivialities. It's the same with something big. Something that has a material effect on a life. You find out you've got cancer. You let it in, let it bite as it will. As it must. *Okay, here it is, this is where I am.* Soft, soft, a flood of peacefulness around the hard fact. How strange this is, but it is so. Doesn't mean you wouldn't rather not have cancer, or that you won't do what you can to get better. Acceptance isn't about that. It's just allowing the truth to fully be what it is, and allowing the peace that comes with the allowing. Then going on from there. Seeing what's next, trying to do something to help the situation.

Resistance comes up, of course, mostly when something challenging or unpleasant or irritating or painful comes down the pike. But really, there's an even-handedness that can come into being even when a thing is felt to be *good*. What is it to be even-handed? to greet everything with this equanimity?

Not to get ecstatic when things go really well. What about that?

This isn't about being a killjoy. A person can discover how much of the feeling-good moments of life take their sustenance from things in life going *well*, and that turns out to be as much a part of the problem as thinking that we can't feel peaceful in the presence of things going badly. It's not that all the gladness has drained out of life. It's that the gladness has been discovered to have its perpetually renewable source within pure awareness – not in things going well. That elemental gladness isn't subject to anything at all. So things can go really well in life, and you might feel great, *but not because things are going well*. And things can fall apart all around you, and you still feel – strangely – pretty good. The feeling-good part is far away from what's gone wrong, or rather, what's gone wrong is like a noise out in the distance.

It's not that it isn't real. It's that it's not as real as the inside-you part.

The thing about calmly accepting whatever comes along, and the flood of peacefulness that brings (whether the accepted thing feels like something bad or something great), is that you get more and more in touch with this awareness in you. Once that's happened, you're in good shape – no matter what comes down the pike.

You Are Not Your Problems

It seems that the troubling thing must be worked out, as understood by the mind. That its terms must be entered into, accepted as given, in order that the decision can be made, the problem resolved, the emotions processed. As if the mental framework of the thing, as it's been constructed, is the only possible place to be in relation to some piece of life, as it's arrived on the scene of present reality.

Then something happens to cause the looking to occur from a different place. Not inside the framework, which has come to feel like the whole world, like reality itself. You didn't even know there *was* a place outside it. You couldn't have imagined having a view of the outside of the walls, because in fact you didn't realize there *were* walls (let alone that you had put them there, having constructed the whole thing with all the hammers and saws inside your head). Until the sudden new view, you thought where you were, in the center of the world you occupied, was the only place to be. That everything in sight, as far as you could see with your mind's lenses, was the extent of reality.

But suddenly, as if you were picked up by a crane, lifted up and out, and set back down again in a whole new place, you are looking from an angle you haven't seen from before. Vaguely the situation looks familiar, you recognize it, only it doesn't look the same because you aren't where you were. You aren't *in* it.

It hasn't changed. You haven't changed, not really. It's just that you've relocated.

You realize, to your stunned amazement, that this perspective always was a possibility. That right along

you've been equipped to see this thing in this way –
this problem that has so gripped you, this real-life
difficulty – which is why you haven't really changed.
You could have seen it this way right along. But you
didn't, until now.

You look at the thing and you see you don't, after all,
have to fix anything – at least, not in order to be okay.
You're standing here, looking, and realizing you
actually feel quite fine, even as you are in unresisting
acknowledgment of the situation. Even though your
issue is ongoing. Inside the structure you are now
looking at, the furnace of angst continues its bright
glow, but here you are, standing out in the dark,
utterly unencumbered, having no idea who you are.

Now that you aren't your problem anymore.

The Uselessness of Trying to Rise Above

My dear elderly friend asked, *How does one manage to mind nothing?* She was wondering this in the context of her recent protracted illness – not serious, but limiting and exhausting.

And now her beloved sister has died. If not-minding is the secret to enduring equanimity, how is it possible to not mind the death of someone you have dearly loved your entire life?

Not minding doesn't mean the absence of grief. It means you don't mind the grief. You allow it to enfold you. You bow to the reality that the person is gone. You don't waste energy on wishing it were otherwise, escaping into a headful of useless if-onlys, or taking refuge in consoling ideas that blunt the terrible pain of loss.

Not minding means you allow to be what is. To mind is to resist, to use the mind to say *no* (whether you're saying no to a death or to a heavy cold). It's using the mind to say *I wish it were otherwise* or *I don't want to feel this* or *I'll be glad when I get past this*. To mind is to want to be other than where you are. It's to set up a conflict within yourself between what's real and what you are comfortable with.

Not minding is being comfortable with what's real. It's surrendering, being willing to be with the truth of a thing, and that includes the willingness to feel the feelings that are running in your veins.

When a person minds something, the mind is being used in a way that (ironically) compounds pain. A rainy day causes pain only if you mind it. With something that's actually painful – like a toothache or grief – minding the pain only intensifies the discomfort.

When someone dear has died, if you try to hold back the tears, or if you comfort yourself with thoughts about how the person is in a better place now, the grief is not being given its due. The purpose of those thoughts is to diminish the pain. Grief that's allowed, without minding the pain, is profoundly cathartic. Grief that's held away is squeezed like a headache into a tight space. It throbs longer and harder than grief (or any pain) given ample space.

The idea of not minding can appear to suggest rising above, tapping into a higher reality. In fact, that picture of not minding takes resistance to the extreme: resisting something so entirely that you distance yourself from it sufficient to have convinced yourself it really doesn't matter. This is a sure-fire recipe for a life of continuing torment. The torment may be low-level, but it will not go away. Suffering will not cease. Sometimes it will erupt from below the neatly packed-down surface, a much more severe pain than the original one would have been, had it been given space at the time.

When it's raining, let it rain. When there is sorrow, be sad. Do not seek refuge in the prospect of a sunny day, or in the picture of the loved one in heaven. Be real with yourself.

The misunderstanding about not minding, in spiritual circles, may come from the observation of great beings, who can seem strangely unaffected by things that are distressing to others. Krishnamurti once said his secret was that he didn't mind anything. Observing him, seeing how unlikely he was to become rattled, a person wanting to emulate the great man might think – *I'm going to try to rise above everything*. As if that might hasten liberation.

This is one of those situations where faking it till you make it is doomed. It's true that once the light has taken over your life, you will not mind things. Few things will stir deep feeling. But until you have been transformed – until your sense of *what you are* has radically shifted – trying to resist pain by using spiritual trickery to "rise above" it is a reliable way to keep liberation at arm's length.

When Krishnamurti's beloved brother died, he descended into an all-consuming grief. He did not attempt to rise above the pain. On a ship at the time he got the news of the death, he closed himself in his room. The others on board could hear the wailing, hour upon hour of wracking grief. Krishnamurti let his heart do the only thing it could do: break. When the door at last opened, those traveling with him would later report the sight of a man strangely calm. At peace. Radiant, in fact. They could not take their eyes from him. When he spoke after that, upon the ship's arrival in India, the clarity and wisdom that came from his lips astounded them. He had come the rest of the way into his fullness.

While someone who has gone beyond identification with ego can indeed experience grief, such a person is unlikely to experience most of the ordinary kinds of emotions (irritation, anger, jealousy). Ordinary life occurrences typically do *not* generate an emotional response. This apparent aloofness can be bewildering to those in the push-and-pull of ego, who *do* experience emotions on a regular basis, who react to trivial things, like a rainy day or getting cut off in traffic. They *do* mind when they get fired, or when the mortgage payment can't be made on time because money is in short supply. But then they look at their spiritual teacher, who (they know) would not mind these things, and because of wanting to be like that person – because of wanting to be spared suffering – they try to convince themselves that they don't mind, when in fact they mind very much. They use their spiritual ideas and aspirations to lie to themselves, to repress their already lively emotions.

This accomplishes two things: it compounds the suffering, and it keeps them from waking up. It compounds the suffering because now there are *two* things causing pain: the thing they dislike (the loss of the job) AND the unacknowledged pain of resistance.

If you mind something but then deny that you mind it – if you try to get yourself to believe you're really fine when you're not – you will stay stuck. You will not wake up by trying to act enlightened. It just does not work.

The way to wake up from the whole mess is to be real with yourself. If you hate that it's raining, go ahead and hate it. Feel how much it hurts to hate the rain. Wallow *(consciously)* in the suffering you are causing yourself. See how the rain is not causing the suffering. *You* are causing it.

Someone tired of suffering does not want to be with the suffering, to dwell in the sensation of it, to become intimate with how it is self-induced. Someone tired of suffering wants to turn *away* from it, not toward it. They look at someone who doesn't suffer, and they think – *I want to be like that.* They think that means "rise above." That isn't it though. When someone wakes up, really wakes up, they have stopped believing they *are* what happens to them. What happens is just . . . what happens. They truly do not mind. It isn't about them. They don't take things personally. They don't have to convince themselves not to mind.

Before the sense of reality has shifted, a person cannot help believing that what happens is, in some sense, about them. They are in the thick of it. Things that happen truly do affect them. And so to pretend it's otherwise – to resist feeling things, to try to rise above, to console self with ideas or aspirations, to escape into meditation or seek out blissful experiences to avoid, distract – it's all an elaborate and useless way of trying to be something you are not. The whole thing will happen over and over again until you have come to face yourself.

If you don't believe me, read Krishnamurti.

If you want to wake up, don't try to be something you are not. This is a real head-scratcher to someone who wants to evolve past where they are. Who is in the thick of it, in the life where what happens has its material effect, but who wants to stop suffering.

When a thing happens, be with it. It's real. You be real too. Acknowledge what you feel. Turn toward the feeling, not away from it. If the thing makes you mad, be real about that. If being mad hurts, be real about that too. Keep being real. (This isn't the same as indulging negative emotions, fanning the flames. Stay conscious through all this.) See how miserable it makes you, how much harm you cause yourself and others. Don't build a wall between yourself and your emotions.

Unless you'd like to stay asleep your entire life.

Sometimes to stop suffering altogether, you have to suffer more. That terrible suffering may be the crisis that brings you to the radical discovery that you are in fact *not* what happens to you. When you have at last seen that, by whatever means, you actually do *not* mind what happens. But until that has happened, don't try to not mind things you really do mind. Feel how much you mind them. How much it hurts to mind. Move *toward* the pain, not away from it. It just might bring you to your knees. Then you won't mind anything anymore.

Meditating All Day Long

Why does a person meditate? What does that mean, *to meditate?* When someone sits for meditation, on a given occasion or as a practice, what expectations are in the picture?

The purpose of meditation is to cultivate inner stillness. To quiet the mind, to observe thought without becoming lost in its content. To meditate is to tune in to immediate physical reality – sensory input, breath, body feelings, the sensation of aliveness. Meditation enables the mind-made impression of time to unwind, so the underlying timelessness can be felt. It opens the door to presence, allowing consciousness itself to be primary.

As a practice, meditation is thought to move along the spiritual life. The hope is that its benefits will extend to improve the experience of daily existence, deepening insights into how the ego functions, bringing spaciousness and well-being into ordinary activities.

Meditation is apart from "regular life." You sit in a quiet place, back straight, eyes closed. You take time for it, setting aside whatever else your day holds. Maybe you take fifteen minutes, maybe an hour. There are countless methods. You may focus on a mantra, a prayer. Perhaps the emphasis is on posture, on the breath, or on sensation in discrete parts of the body. The focus may be on the reception of sounds and other sensations in their raw, unfiltered form, without label or judgment. The orientation to thought may be a primary meditation practice.

Devoted meditators sometimes go on retreats, days or weeks or months away from the usual routine and setting of life. Typically on retreat there are long periods of meditation. Re-entry into one's normal circumstances can be challenging, the return to family and work being an invitation to slip back into familiar limiting patterns. The retreat itself can stir up enormous discomfort: the sustained silence and inner focus may bring a practitioner to confront difficult truths about the self. Even if a retreat is the setting for painful revelation, the time there feels authentic and essential in a way ordinary life may not.

Like meditation done at home, a retreat usually feels conspicuously different from daily life. This *apartness* has a lot to do with its appeal. A retreat is a respite, an opportunity to regroup, to be restored. It's a way to be with kindred spirits, away (maybe) from people at home who can be challenging to inner well-being, people for whom the spiritual life may not be central.

A line is drawn between retreat and life, between meditation and ordinary daily experience. A gong sounds, indicating beginning or end. You get in your car and head to the retreat, then back home. There's a transition, the perception that meditation is one thing and life another.

* * * * *

This is not about trying to talk you out of meditating. For goodness' sake, if you're moved to formal meditation, at home or elsewhere, do it. What this is about is noticing the distinction you may make between meditation and life. It's about discovering what can be learned by exploring the apparent difference between the two. It's about finding doors where you thought there were only walls. It's about life becoming a joy, not a burden. Not something to survive until you can get back on your cushion, back to the retreat center. Or maybe you see life as a dulling but comfortable refuge from the constraints of what meditation is "supposed" to be.

This is about ceasing to see life and meditation as distinct from one another.

* * * * *

When the gong rings (or the timer on your smartphone), signaling the end of meditation, what happens inside you? See what you notice about your muscles, your breath. Does your body shift? relax? tense? What goes on in your mind? Do you become self-conscious? There may be a feeling of relief, of letting down your guard. The release of some kind of subtle effort or tension, the welcome sense that now something (anything!) different can happen. The familiar machinery of the self can start up, the resumption of the comforting patter in your head. You can get up and go to the bathroom. You can encounter other people. *Whew.*

If you feel peaceful coming out of meditation, you may try to "make it last," to extend the equanimity into ordinary activity (and then feel defeated when that effort fails).

During meditation, do you find yourself wondering how much time is left? Perhaps there's a sense of whether you're "doing it right." Do you feel restless, itchy to return to the comfort of the familiar momentum? When it's over, maybe you secretly welcome the return to the self you're used to being, even as the spiritual adept in you knows that very self to be the source of suffering.

Is meditation a break from life, an escape? Maybe you
wish it would save you from yourself, from life. Some
people meditate to cultivate blissful experiences,
preferring mystical states to ordinary experience,
imagining some greater reality is being touched. But
the vast majority of life is not spent in meditation or
on retreat. Whether you're still bound to the ego or
blessedly free of it, life consists largely of ordinary
experience. Life is lived with your eyes open, with
your body in motion, with things to do, a steady
stream of things coming at you (only some of them
pleasant).

When you're on your way home from a retreat, do you
dread getting pulled back into patterns of negativity?
Is there relief at the prospect of return to the
comforting setting and routine, to the numbing
lullaby of unconsciousness?

* * * * *

None of this is "bad." If that's where you go with it –
to feeling guilty, embarrassed, inadequate – don't
bother lingering there. It's a waste of your precious
life (and anyhow, it's the ego that feels these things).
Instead, use those inner twinges to go deeper, to look
at beliefs underlying them. Unobserved, those ideas
create a prison. But when you lift them into conscious
awareness and explore their ramifications, a door
opens to your next adventure in self-discovery.
Whereas those unquestioned beliefs have kept you
repeating useless patterns, now that you're looking at
them, they lose substance. A new freedom becomes
possible.

When you consider what your ordinary life is like –
what you feel like when engaged in work,
communicating, relating, focused on projects, during

down time – does it appear that the You in regular-life mode is different from who you are during meditation? Does the difference seem inevitable? If you tell yourself (consciously or unconsciously) that inner stillness is inconsistent with the motion, outer focus, and busyness of ordinary life, examine this belief. See how it traps you in familiar patterns and actually encourages unconsciousness (because "why bother?").

Perhaps you believe that being engaged and productive inevitably negates presence, putting you at the mercy of the mind-driven ego. See how these ideas limit you. Notice how they exaggerate the significance of meditation and retreats, as a necessary refuge, a counter-balance to the overwhelming forces of life.

If you tell yourself that regular life and equanimity are at odds, something in you registers it's natural (maybe even unavoidable) that you'll become constricted during "regular life." This supports the ongoing illusion that you need to change into some other sort of person, before you can know your true nature. The cycle of useless effort continues, getting you nowhere.

Do your times of meditation seem more "spiritual" than your time at work, engaging with your partner or family members, cleaning your living space? Can you imagine that you could, in effect, be "meditating" all day, even at work, in encounter with someone?

* * * * *

What do you suppose it's like to be completely friendly with daily existence? Even as you know things will keep coming from out of left field, that there will be difficulties, that you are not in charge. Imagine life not being contrary to the inner stillness sought in meditation. In-motion, eyes-open life! What would it be to live – to do things, make progress, engage in conversation – without the mind's opinionated chatter? To really *be* in life, this moment of it, and yet not to be defined or burdened by it?

If you're thinking – okay, maybe this is how it is for somebody no longer identified with the ego, *but it isn't me* – hang on. That very assumption keeps the boundary solidly drawn between meditation and life. It makes you lazy, neglectful of *this moment* and *this one*. It keeps you from remembering to notice – *in the context of any real-life experience* – that it's possible to become still inside, to feel what it is to be. Simply to *be*.

It's possible to pause in the middle of any moment and see that the thought you've been "lost" in is just a thought. And then see how the stillness comes. See how you become refreshed, able to bring attention to what your senses are presently offering to you. *Mid-stream* you are refreshed, just as you are on your cushion.

Opportunities abound. Meditation everywhere! Simply by bringing attention to the thing you're doing right now (*not* doing one thing and thinking about the next thing, or about whether you like what's happening at present) – just by *being here* with what is – you can feel a door open, as surely as you feel your mind grow quiet when you sit on a cushion, eyes shut, and let your muscles unwind.

Because we're busy, and things are in constant flux, it appears that life is in motion, and we are carried along in its merciless force. Ordinary awareness has us convinced that we're moving "through time." Part of the reason meditation can be delicious is it feels like permission to stop, to rest. But any time you stop, in the middle of ordinary activity – a few seconds will do it! – and feel what it feels like to be you right now, in your body, heart, and mind, you can become aware of the stillness of the present moment. *It's always here, if only we will pause and notice.*

Present-moment reality, when the attention is there, when there is no resistance, is a fine thing on which to meditate. (And if you notice there *is* resistance, meditate on *that*, as it is occurring.) Isn't the breath always happening? If you pause to notice your breath, as you might in meditation, can you find it? Is there sensation in your body, always? Doesn't your body go anywhere you go, your sense receptors always there? Can't your eyes and ears tune in to what's *right here?* At lunch time, if you allow your tongue to linger over this bite in the mouth, do you see how the morning's "problems" dissolve into spacious stillness, into taste?

The real benefit of a meditation practice is not figuring out how to extend its peacefulness past the ringing of the gong. It's about learning to discover the peace anew – freshly, in *this* moment, in the middle of the busy day. So much more truly renewing than looking back wistfully to the ease you felt coming out of morning meditation, lamenting your perennial inability to "make it last."

Isn't the sweetness of meditation about *attention* – to this breath, this moment, this sensation of being alive? What makes you think that isn't constantly available, in the middle of anything? The shocking truth that sometimes erupts in the silence of a retreat – can that not come in the middle of a work day, in the aftermath of an argument with a co-worker? Can such an experience, considered in the light of

awareness, not become your teacher, a door opening
to insight and eventual freedom?

If you have the habit of believing that certain ways of
being simply are not possible in Regular Life, that
ordinary experience is inconsistent with being present
and self-aware, you are maintaining the very prison
that you'd swear you long to become free of.
Meditation will continue to be a break from the
imprisoning norm. Life will keep seeming like the
thing to be tamed, triumphed over, or escaped.

Meditate all day! Sometimes during breakfast,
sometimes at work, sometimes on a cushion. Sitting at
a red light, waiting for the elevator, standing in line at
Starbucks. Meanwhile, when it seems to be impossible
to grow still inside, to bring attention to one thing,
instead of just getting frustrated or feeling
inadequate, do some gentle digging in your heart and
mind. See what you deeply believe about what's
possible and what's not, about what's in the way,
what's necessary to become still, self-aware. *Question
every assumption.* Take nothing for granted as "the
truth," just because it's what you've believed until
now.

Let doors open. If you think there's a wall separating
life from meditation, from retreats, run your hands
over the wall and feel for cracks in the rigid belief
structures. Maybe those cracks are doors.

* * * * *

If you sit for meditation, enter into it with your whole
body and mind and heart. It can only be a blessing (so
long as you don't try to direct it, or enter it full of
expectation). Let meditation take you in its arms. Do

your part to show up for it, but realize it has its own wisdom.

If you think you aren't meditating "right," move your attention from the exhausting effort to improve and see if you can simply be more truly present to life itself. Feel the difference between receptivity and effort. See what happens when you stop trying so hard and instead let yourself be soft, vulnerable to this moment of life, willing to be with whatever is there. Allowing life to be your teacher.

If you love the restfulness of sitting on a cushion with your eyes closed, after you've gotten up and the day is moving along, notice how any time you pause in the middle of the action – even during something unpleasant – you can feel yourself back on that cushion. The stillness moves with you, as you move. It goes everywhere you go. It didn't stay on the cushion. It didn't flee when your eyes opened.

You Don't Need to Change

If only you could see this. Stop trying to change yourself. You are so busy trying to change yourself (suffer less, be less attached, become enlightened) that you can't see the forest for the trees. Some of the really huge, light-blocking, preoccupying trees are your efforts to improve – as if the one you're working to improve were who you *are!*

What's needed is *not* for you to change your familiar self (the one that longs to awaken, the one that hurts, that is dissatisfied with itself). What's needed is for you to see that that person is not what you deeply are. Trying to improve the person that isn't what you deeply are – believing this could wake you up – is like planting a bunch of new trees in the forest, further obscuring the blinding light that is your very nature. It is (to switch metaphors) scoring points for the other side.

Do you see?

It is as if there are two of you. As long as you believe that you *are* your egoic self, for all practical purposes, there are two of you. The self that is capable of believing it needs to change is your egoic self (however much it may entertain itself with thoughts of wanting to awaken). What you need to do, rigorously, is remember that there is always another of you available in each moment – that you can (as it were) step inside that other awareness, the one that is *not* hurting, not trying to change, not believing it must awaken.

This is the only truly useful thing to do.

You may be ready to see this, to actually do it (sometimes anyhow). You may not be. When you are ready, you will see it. You will experience the truth of it, that there is another awareness inside you *already* that is able to step outside the turmoil, in a given moment, and observe your struggling self, the one that believes it needs to change.

Meanwhile, if you are not able to step outside and look at yourself in a moment of life, smack in the middle of some kind of angst, *at least* do this: stop believing that your egoic mind can somehow bring about a useful change in itself that will move you toward awakening. The oft-stated idea that you already *are* that which you seek isn't just blah-blah-blah. When you focus all your effort on trying to improve your egoic self, you are turning away from this truth. (Just because you can't yet see its reality doesn't mean it isn't so.)

Anytime you are in torment, even subtle torment, and you notice it, instead of trying to "fix" the problem, instead of judging yourself for being so unawake, just step gently to the side of the whole thing and look at it. Look at yourself feeling this thing, thinking these thoughts. That other looker, that un-caught-up observer, is always *(always)* there, available, if only you will remember its presence. You may not always be able readily to step inside it, assuming its perspective. But at the very least you must remember that it's possible.

This is the whole thing.

Stepping outside and looking at yourself in this moment is not the same thing as escape. Escaping is turning on the TV, chanting, meditating or doing yoga to try to bring on an ecstatic experience, mixing a drink, talking to yourself about how "this isn't who I really am." These things accomplish nothing to demonstrate to you that you are something very different from the one who needs to escape. Instead, stay where you are. Stay in the moment – the feeling – you are in. But *also* step outside and watch it happening. Realize that the one who is doing the looking is not experiencing discomfort, is not needing escape. Is not needing to wake up! Because it already is awake. This moment, just now, awakeness is feeling its reality. It doesn't mean you're "awake for good." Never mind that. Stop thinking about that.

Do you see?

Don't get lazy. Don't stop remembering that this is available to you, this location outside the drama. One time you will find yourself entirely outside, watching your regular self, and you will say *Oh my God, THIS is what I am!* "This" being the looker. You may know this for just a second. Just a fleeting, delicious, utterly peaceful few moments. Don't (really) say, *If only this can last.* Just be there. Later (maybe ten seconds later) you will be back in the muck, having completely forgotten. It's okay! The instant you notice you've forgotten, just step back outside and look. Forget trying to make it last. When you have that kind of thought, realize it's just the ego-mind doing the only thing it knows how to do.

You may be thinking *Well, but doesn't my regular-life stuff matter?* Or you may be thinking *What's the relationship between the regular-life stuff and this other perspective?* It's only the mind that feels the need to sort this out. When you grow accustomed to stepping outside a moment in which you're feeling very attached to something, when you give yourself the peace and delight of experiencing your "other" self, then the regular-life stuff sorts itself out. It isn't your business to answer the mind's pesky questions. Just trust that your really huge, utterly non-attached self is saturated with wisdom that is dying to leak into your regular life, and if you give it half a chance, it will do that.

One thing that happens, the more you do this, is that you (bit by bit) stop believing that the regular-life You is what you most deeply are. So you are able to "hold it" more lightly, because there isn't so (bloody) much invested in its upkeep. Yes, you will still tend what needs tending (very tenderly).

The point is, you don't have to figure everything out. Something in you (that outside looker) knows this.

When you are hurting, or feeling very unawake, or dissatisfied with yourself, instead of saying "I've got to change" or "I've got to get enlightened," instead of those (useless) things, do this: even as you are immersed in the present-moment feeling of discomfort, dislike of self, etc., step outside of the whole thing and look at yourself. Neutrally, without judgment. (If there's judgment, you're not outside the whole thing. Get farther out.)

The entire problem is that you believe you are your egoic self, the regular-life person, the one that suffers (and wants to wake up). That is the whole thing. When you step outside and look at it, you are reminding yourself of what you really are.

What You Can Do to Wake Up: Not This

The longing to become free of suffering, to rest in peaceful well-being, gives rise to various approaches, not all of which bear fruit. Here are three common ones:

- Work on the familiar self, in the hope that it will improve all the way to awakening

- Pursue a heightened experience or state

- Master spiritual ideas and terminology (equating mental understanding with visceral knowing)

All of these approaches are misguided. They are undertaken by the ego, aimed at improving itself. *As if the ego could be perfected.*

If so much of what passes for spiritual work is wheel-spinning, what might a person profitably focus on instead?

The seed of fruitful effort lies in the question *What am I?* When everything changes, the answer to that question is different from what it was before. Not the intellectually known answer but the one that comes viscerally. You literally no longer experience *what you are* the way you used to.

(In case you're telling yourself that you already "know" you aren't your ego, please realize this is probably a *mental* knowing – and not all that transformative, as you may have noticed. Only bodied knowing indicates real change. When the change in perspective has occurred, you *experience* yourself differently.)

When you look back to *before*, you will see (such a revelation!) that what you once absolutely believed to be *you* was just a hodgepodge of memories, conditioning, personality, physical features, stories, ideas and beliefs, and fleeting emotional states. All of it one big unwieldy blob, having enormous weight and stickiness and emitting a foul odor. This blob was carried along in the suitcase of your mind through every adventure, as if without it all, you would cease to be.

It sure did *seem* like what you really were. Now, relieved of it, you can hardly believe you once invested it with reality, exhausting yourself trying to make the thing workable and impressive.

After everything changes, really just *one* thing has changed: your sense of identity has shifted from all of that to something else. The blob-filled suitcase has been abandoned by the side of the road. The something else is not as easy to describe as the prior mess, where the familiar satisfaction and suffering have flourished.

It's easier to portray the *after* by saying what's missing. Time no longer feels real to you. It doesn't occur to you to resist, or to make up a story about anything. You've stopped grousing. No matter what, you're content. Since all of that other stuff about "you" no longer has substance, you – the newly-experienced you – cannot be harmed or threatened or made to feel insecure. You no longer have the machinery to get your dander up, or to be embarrassed, or to feel especially pleased with yourself. Your mind is quiet, unless you need to think about something.

You no longer take seriously that person you once thought you were.

What does it feel like *you* are, then? Consciousness. Spaciousness. Beingness.

It's unmistakable that this exquisite reality has been here all along. That you have come home. There is nothing new about it. It's just newly . . . *recognized.* Occupied.

Your sense of self includes present-moment reality – the now – whatever that may be. You don't feel separate from what's happening. The reason it doesn't occur to you to resist anything is that you don't experience reality as if it were "over there" and "you" are here, making assessments about it. (The assessor has gone missing.)

* * * * *

The compelling question to pose to yourself is *What am I?* What do you experience yourself as being?

The question is not *How can I improve myself?* or *How can I experience higher consciousness (or get it to last)?* or *What more do I need to learn?*

As for pursuing the longed-for condition, rest from that. It's the ego that's seeking a certain kind of imagined pleasant experience. Consciousness itself wants for nothing. Only the ego can want. When wanting comes, recognize it for what it is: *there it is, the ego doing its thing.* Then leave it be. Don't let it lead you around by the nose.

The memory of a period of blissful or peaceful consciousness can become a torment, a thing to attempt to re-create. You may have an idea of what it would be like to get beyond ego, and you've made it your goal to "get there." It's safe to assume that your imagining of freedom is no predictor of what it will actually be like. See that the image in your head is a thought, nothing more. You are pursuing an idea, and it's located in some possible future, which has no existence independent of your picture of it.

A huge amount of misdirected spiritual work is aimed at trying to fix the ego, to make it more comfortable. The idea of "working on yourself," that cherished project of the self-help industry, seems to have infected contemporary spirituality.

The ego, for many, has become spiritualized. It's cloaked in spiritual affectation, adorned in practices and lofty ideas that thrive radically disconnected from real life. The spiritual ego takes on the tortured vocabulary of nonduality – "the character," "this body-mind" – as if the scrupulous avoidance of the first-person pronoun will engender the experience of no-self. Intent on awakening, a well-meaning person will assume a spiritual name, give up meat, adopt a certain lingo or practice, affect "sweetness and light" as a way to keep a lid on anger and fear. Denial flourishes like an invasive plant form. People wonder why they get stuck.

If you are taking offense at this, let a light come on. The "you" that's capable of taking offense (like the you that's cultivated a spiritual identity) is not what you deeply are. Only the ego can be offended. As it's said in *A Course in Miracles,* "Nothing real can be threatened." If you feel threatened by what someone says or does, *by definition* what's enlivened is your ego.

Don't try to change your ego or cultivate a certain identity. Rather than judging the misdeeds of your mind-made self, simply become acquainted with how it operates. See the strength of identification with your history and beliefs. See how easily you get sucked into your thoughts, as if they were the truth. As if they were *you*.

If you focus on trying to eliminate your negativity, weed out your cherished beliefs, peel away your conditioning, manage your anger, or distance yourself from your difficult history, your precious attention is being squandered. What you're trying to do is spruce up your familiar self. As if it could be improved all the way to awake.

Do you see the folly of this?

There's nothing "wrong" with taking on a spiritual identity . . . so long as you don't imagine it will set you free. No matter how the ego is clothed, how it dances or speaks, underneath it's still its same reactive, fearful, defensive self. That wolf in sheep's clothing, you might say. A spiritual identity is no better than any other kind of identity. An identity that's got to do with higher consciousness seems to set it apart (above), but this is just one more illusion – an especially deceptive one. It's around every corner, waiting to trick you once more.

Your fundamental nature – that which you long to dwell in, as – has no identity at all. Any attempt to embody its enormity in a name, a mere word, is inevitably reductive. No collection of ideas can hope to account for it. You're much better off ceasing to maintain any identity. Only then can it get quiet enough inside to sense what you are, apart from all definition.

Don't let the apparently spiritual nature of your familiar self deceive you into supposing this is anything but another project of the ego. The wolf may have changed its clothing, but the animal is the same.

It's the most natural thing in the world to want to soothe or strengthen the ego. The deep motivator is to feel better. (This – not the longing to know the truth – is what leads most people to the spiritual life.) Since the ego is both the cause and the victim of suffering, it looks as though "fixing" the ego would be the way to suffer less.

* * * * *

The real answer comes alive at a more fundamental level. Investigate the enduring impression that the ego is what you *are*. It's the *identification* with ego that keeps the suffering going. That identification must occur first, *before* the familiar pattern of thought-induced suffering can continue to run. If you don't mistake the ego for what you are – if you don't take it seriously – it will unwind quite naturally. It will no longer so enthrall you.

To linger in the ego itself, to focus on "improving" it, is only to continue to feed and clothe and house it. *As if it were the ultimate reality.* As if it could hope to traverse the vast distance between itself and whatever is beyond it.

When the ego gets your attention, and you become dissatisfied (frustrated, afraid, whatever), instead of going where you usually go, which is to try to improve your reaction, thought patterns, emotions, or make an intention to "do better" in the future, simply remind yourself that this thing that suffers, tries harder, gets discouraged, and intends, is not what you are. When you let it engross you, when you believe its thoughts with an eye to solving its "problems," you are saying you believe it's what you are, that it's worthy of attention.

It is not fixable, not radically. The level on which it's fixable is psychological, not existential. (Psychological improvements are not worthless, but they will not set you free.)

The ego does not evolve into unencumbered consciousness. *Beingness is here already*, in spite of the ego, entirely independent of its force field. Your true nature has nothing whatever to do with the concerns of the mind-made self. All that changes is that at some point one stops feeling real and the other assumes vitality, like an organ that's always been with you but is only now getting blood to it.

The illusion that you can improve all the way to waking up is rooted in the illusion that you are not already the longed-for thing. You have to believe you're not already *That* in order to suppose that fixing your ego could lead you to awakeness. The whole thing is merely a perception problem. You don't need time to fix your ego. (There isn't enough time in eternity to fix an ego.) If there's a need for time, it's so you can discover what you've been distracted from all along. Not so you can "attain" something. *You've already attained it. You just can't see it.* This is because the thing you think you are has been holding all of your attention, your entire life.

Trying to improve your ego may result in superficial improvements to the invented self, but it will never haul you out of the world of illusion. The ego does not become lighter until it ultimately awakens. Yet this fond hope is what drives many a seeker. *The ego does*

not awaken. The primary goal of the ego, ever and
always, is self-preservation. You will never convince
the ego to get out of its own way, to walk to the edge of
a cliff and step off.

What you wake up to is that you are not (and never
were) your ego. The problem is not that your ego
suffers; it's that you mistake it for what you are.

Focus on the nature of what you appear to be. Become
intensely curious about how this *you* functions. How
it is generated, how it maintains and defends and
asserts and consoles itself. What it clings to for self-
definition. So that you can recognize it for what it is,
immediately, each time it stirs itself – instead of
engaging with its picture of reality, instead of cringing
at its antics and trying to make it behave better.

What you're learning about – a truly fruitful endeavor
– is what you are *not*.

As you observe this invented self functioning, as you
see your investment in it, ceaselessly remind yourself
– *Not this*. It – the truth of what I am – is not this.
Whatever it is, it isn't this blob, this ceaseless loop of
stories, this emotional stew, a head full of spiritual
ideas. However well-meaning it might all be, however
noble its aspirations. *This isn't it.*

Nor is it this. You are getting a mountain's worth of
evidence of what you are not, even as it continues to
enthrall.

At least don't score points for the other side. Stop
telling yourself that all this stuff inside the suitcase is
what a human life is meant to be about, the thing
we're all here to discover. Keep reminding yourself:

Not this, not this. Don't get sucked in (for the millionth time) to trying to remold your ego.

See how much you *want* to identify with the familiar self. It will constantly fool you into thinking *surely this is real.* At some point the thought will come . . . *Well, if THIS isn't what I really am, then what AM I?* Which may be scary.

But now you are standing in front of the door that's been waiting for you. So patiently, all your precious life.

* * * * *

What am I? This is what you ultimately come to. The way to prepare yourself to pose that question – not intellectually, but in your body, existentially – is to consistently recognize the ego for what it is and to withdraw attention from its concerns. You must be *pressed* to the question *What am I?* It's only by the devoted *Not this, not this* that you can become clear of all the distraction of the suffering ego that has appeared to be fixable, that has pursued a certain kind of experience or "state."

Nisargadatta's teacher told him, "You are not what you take yourself to be. Find out what you are. Watch the sense 'I am.' Find your real Self."

Here's Nisargadatta's description of what happened: "This brought an end to the mind; in the stillness of the mind I saw myself as I am – unbound. I used to sit for hours together, with nothing but the 'I am' in my mind, and soon peace and joy and a deep all-embracing love became my normal state. In it all disappeared – myself, my Guru, the life I lived, the world around me. Only peace remained and an unfathomable silence."

One fine moment of electric stillness, it will dawn on you what you actually *are*. To prepare the ground for this revelation, devote yourself to the scrupulous, gutsy recognition of what you are *not*.

Watch What Really Happens

What appears to be a single multifaceted response to a moment of life is, if you look closely, several steps that occur in rapid succession. They happen in a particular order. Every time. The steps come fast like falling dominoes, so the impression is that they occur concurrently. As if all of a piece.

But slow it down – look at it in slow motion – and you will see there are in fact discrete stages. And it matters. Oh, it does matter. Discovering this in your own experience has everything to do with innocence: what it is to encounter any moment of life with freshness, unburdened by the freight of accumulated experience and belief. It's what it is to be really alive, really *here,* without experiencing everything through the contorted lenses of the ego.

I am no brain scientist. This is something I've discovered directly, by observing what happens in my experience. A scientist could doubtless do a better job of naming these three fleeting stages of awareness, but I'll describe them the best I can.

First, there is perception. The senses detect something out there (or something in here, if the momentary experience being given attention is inside the body). This first step is on the level of pure sensation. Data collection. Perhaps a felt response in the body. Even if it's a moderate physical pain in your body, you haven't yet come to the point of saying *Uh-oh, I wonder what's going on.* Language and concept have not kicked in.

Immediately following that, the mind begins its accustomed processing. Here is where the names for things come into awareness, where previously learned information is stirred to life. You are reminded of categories, of connections between things, of causality and pattern. Here is where you become able to anticipate what might be next, to see ramifications. This processing occurs without evaluation or emotional charge. Nothing, yet, is seen as good or bad. It's a matter of fact, at this point – at least, as best the mind can determine. It isn't about *you*, at this stage.

The third step is where things get interesting. Where the trouble often starts. The ego gets busy, with the support of the mind, making up a story, going into resistance, fear, anger, explanation. Interpreting in terms of *you*, figuring out whether this moment of life is welcome or a nuisance, why it's happening, what it might portend for you or another. This is where investment starts up, where emotion gets generated, in response to the ego-mind's take on what's happening.

If what the senses detect, at the initial stage, is immediate physical threat, the animal body that you fundamentally *are* simply responds in the way it must to keep alive, bypassing steps two and three, or perhaps postponing them until (if) the crisis is survived. The name for the threat does not need to come to you in order for you to brace yourself, or to turn and flee. At a life-threatening moment, there is doubtless a feeling in the body, having to do with adrenaline, probably among other physical processes.

What we're looking at here is the 99.9% of life where there is no one coming at you with a hatchet or a truck, but the inside of you is behaving and feeling as though there *were*.

If you watch, you will see that these three things – perception, mental fathoming, and ego-processing – while they appear to come simultaneously, in fact are distinct, and occur *in that order*. Every single time. It has been this way forever.

If some night you come upon a building on fire – say, a building in a town you're driving through on a trip far from home, a place unknown to you – at the sight of the flames sending sparks into the black sky, the roar of the conflagration (your senses captivated), what may ride into your body with the visual and auditory and olfactory data may be a rush of something like . . . *excitement* . . . at the unprocessed physical spectacle of it. This happens *before* your mind has kicked in, reminding you that this fire represents destruction and possible loss of life. (You may have noticed this feeling of excitement even with a building closer to home, but in that case the original felt response was quickly eclipsed by the mind and ego rushing in with responsibility, guilt, concern.)

Right about now, you may be saying *Who cares?*

* * * * *

I am wanting to account for the peaceful well-being, the radical innocence, of someone whose sense of self has changed from what it once was. What is the experience of ordinary moments like, after the change?

The senses operate (wonderfully, better than before, it seems, since you're really *there* for a thing). The mind may or may not engage gears; it may remain quite still in the face of sensory aliveness, with no rush to name a thing, to understand what's happening. Just an impression of movement and color, maybe; something happening to the skin. An *animal* sort of encounter, primarily physical. If the mind *does* want (or need) to engage, in a way to process what's happening, to understand what the senses are detecting, it does so effortlessly, functioning clearly.

But here's the point: it isn't *inevitable* that the mind will engage. It is possible – for any of us, ever – to linger at the sensory. Before words, before meaning.

And here's the juicier point: moving on to the third step, the *What do I think about this?,* is far out on the spectrum. Certainly not inevitable. Seldom gone to, in fact.

This is what accounts for the radical restfulness: that the third step almost never occurs, and when it does, only when you've asked it to. (And then, because you have no machinery for resisting, whatever happens there isn't experienced as a problem.) Even the second step, where mental processing occurs, isn't inevitable.

The rest is profound. You're just *here,* aware. Not wearing yourself out with processing.

But in momentary life as ordinarily experienced, these three steps are not even recognized as discrete developments. Coming to observe what's actually going on opens a door. To put it mildly.

The idea is not to try to discipline self, as if one "should" stop short of the third step, or maybe even the second. It doesn't work that way. But just to notice the blur of dominoes – to observe the mad rush to opinion, worry, desire. To see that something happened *before* the ego got busy. Just watch how it happens. Come to notice the order of things. Along the way, observe how you've been under the impression that it all happens at once, as if contained in a single body of momentary experience. It just isn't so. Find out for yourself.

Watch what happens then. Don't try to *make* it happen. Just watch.

Suffering: That Extra Something

Someone observed that suffering is what happens when a person adds something on. Suffering is generated when thoughts are piled on to a challenging life development, or a loss, or physical discomfort. Each of which, in its essence, may be inherently painful, absorbing of a certain kind of attention. But there needn't be suffering.

Suffering is what occurs when the next step is taken. When a rainy day isn't allowed to be simply a rainy day, but grousing is piled on to it. It's the uncomfortable pressure that occurs when resistance starts up. When the loss of a job isn't allowed to be its plain self – the end of a job – but is weighted down by the story of looming disaster, or the idea of being a failure as a person.

Life stuff needn't lead to the secondary step of suffering. While difficult life developments are inevitable, suffering *is not*. (Now there's a radical idea for you.)

Such a waste of pain. The layered-on misery of pointlessly wishing things were other than they are, or going back over how a thing could have been prevented. What is it to just *be with* the difficulty, unburdened of the story you might have drummed up? It's to accept the truth of the situation. It's to feel what the circumstances stir in your body, without going into your head to try to avoid the hurt, or to generate a consoling narrative, or one full of blame and regret.

Life is not going to be pain-free. Loss visits at intervals. Things don't always go the way we'd like. We get sick. People die. Is it not supposed to hurt to live a rich human life?

But aren't these things suffering? *No,* not when they're allowed to be as they are, without that extra step that occurs when thought moves in to handle what's happened. To allow grief in its fullness, without mental handling, can be an experience of vast tenderness. A breaking heart feels exquisitely alive, even while the pain might be breathtaking.

So it's a matter of seeing the difference between the "clean" pain of being alive, and the layered-on agony (pointless, unnecessary) of wishing life were otherwise, or trying to escape the truth, or making it into a story with justifications and assurances about a better future.

When nothing is added on to life, but it is fully allowed to be as it is, then you don't suffer. You feel alive, even during the times of pain. As you continue on, you travel lightly, not carrying the burden of what's happened. Life is ever fresh. Even when it hurts.

Living Without Mental Management

Because you are alive, something is happening, always. Part of what's happening, unceasingly, is what's going on inside you (often in reaction to what's going on out there). But you aren't always aware of that inner reality, not from the vantage point outside of it, almost as if it were happening to somebody else.

In a moment of self-awareness, you are neutrally observing yourself feel or think something. Or maybe there is a physical sensation, or sensory impression coming at you from the outside, and you see yourself experiencing that. At such a moment you are conscious.

The question is, what is it like to *stay* in the experience, its stripped-down self, without introducing context? Without putting a mental frame around it? Without giving it a name (*loneliness, anger, stupidity*), without touching someplace along a scale (*good, bad, unfortunate*). Without generating a conceptual framework for the momentary reality: *This is me being my father's son,* or *Typical me, a Virgo through and through.*

Automatically we do this. But we don't have to. A thing *could* just be felt, experienced, let be its stripped-down self, without enlarging it somehow via mental context.

We live inside our interpretations of things. This is living at a remove from life.

If what you hunger for is validation, or solace, or what gets called self-love, then you'll take refuge in some kind of mental management of what's happening. You'll use the story to protect yourself from the spontaneous experience of what-is. Alternatively, if what you hunger for is freedom, you'll forgo the story, the label, the attempt to account for. Instead you'll live in the direct experience of reality, as it's presently occurring, including whatever you may be feeling in response.

What we want to be free from is not life but the mental overlays (and the painful emotions generated by them). The mental management seems to come into the picture, almost as if it couldn't be otherwise.

But it could. We do it on purpose (to protect ourselves from life). This occurs almost always below the level of conscious awareness. But once you look, you can see it occurring, and you can see that it's deliberate.

It turns out to be such a relief *not* to do it. When you don't mediate experience with thought, it's like you just got dipped into life, saturated in experience itself. It feels good to do this, even when life is feeling bad. It feels good to have the unmediated moment, the unexplained, unresisted morsel of life.

We want to assemble a narrative about ourselves. It's comforting, maybe even entertaining. But it puts bubble wrap around us, between us and life.

The thing is, it's necessary to go into the head to make sense of something. Reflecting on something, explaining something to self, passing judgment, is not a bodied experience. It's a mental experience (often leading to an emotional one). Life has blood flowing through it. It's warm or chilly, or thrilling, or painful.

You could do a comparison of how it is, the two ways. Forgo the mental component, just a time or two, to see how it feels. Versus what happens when you let a story develop, experiencing the mind's rendering of reality. The tendency, then, is to stay stuck in the story.

The mind comes in, often, as a kind of buffer. That bubble wrap. A way to dull the sensation. (Kind of like living life inside a condom.) See how doing it the other way means pain might be more keenly felt, absent the consoling, numbing construct brought into the picture . . . but also, see something else. How the fuller experience of feeling enables you to move on without any of it clinging to you. You aren't as likely to haul around the experience that you really fully felt, that you let be its uninterpreted self. The experience has its momentary effect, you feel really alive (even if also sad or embarrassed), and then the next thing happens, and you are able to experience it wholly, authentically, untainted by what came before.

This is what it is to be conscious. Which is to say, alive.

Outside the Box

The absorbing thing that present-day life is – life as it just now appears to you, what's getting attention, what stirs worry, desire, all of it – that thing, collectively, is in a box. We don't normally experience it that way, as being contained, because it doesn't occur to the ordinary mind that there's anything *but* what's in the box. That's because we are *in* the box. Actually, each of us *is* the box, each our own box, since everything that makes up "my present life" seems to be "me." There is little to no awareness that something of ourselves could be outside the box.

What happens, when the switch is flipped, is that you suddenly have the sense of being outside all of it. You are looking at it – looking at *you* and your so-called life – from some point outside the familiar orientation.

Meanwhile, until the switch flips, it appears, from within the box, that what merits attention is all the stuff in it. The issues that need resolving, the things you're doing, taking care of. Things you're keeping going. Like your self.

When somebody becomes intent on improving things – losing weight, getting a better job, fixing the relationship, earning more money, even becoming more self-aware – that intention is occurring inside the box. Even spiritual seekers are doing what they're doing in there. They may get frustrated, or despairing, or proud of their progress, and all of that is in there too.

Meanwhile, outside the box there is the whole universe of awareness (the real you, where nothing at all needs improving).

The tendency is to think if you keep working, just try a little harder, things will get better.

The impression that's going, the entire time, the energy source that keeps it all going, even through the periods of discouragement, and even desolation, is that you *are* the person that wants things to get better. That is capable of improving.

Meanwhile, the vastness outside the box is what you *really* are. The endless space on every side of the box can see that you (the you you keep imagining yourself to be, the one that can have something wrong with it, that can succeed or fail) are spinning your wheels.

Spiritual seekers tend to think that they can work their way out of the box. As if there were a door. They will say they understand this whole thing about the apparent self, and that they know they are something beyond that. But if they *really* understood that – got it not just mentally but in all their other organs – they would no longer be in the box, trying to feel around in the dark for the door that isn't there.

When the switch flips, it has dawned on you that you aren't what's in the box. The sense of identity has completely changed. You get the whole thing. You see, with the clarity of a thousand suns, that all your effort to bring about a good life, to fix yourself and others and the world, occurred within a tiny room, which felt like the whole world to you.

You suddenly appear very poignant to yourself.

Someone will say, okay, so what do I do? If the kind of effort I've been investing isn't going to get me anywhere, what do I do instead?

I know that question is there. I'm running out of any inclination to try to answer it. There just isn't a good answer, because the asker of the question is (alas) inside the box, living in the impression that the necessary thing is to feel around in the dark for a door.

There is no door.

But remember: you are outside the box already. Always have been. Never mind that you aren't conscious of this, in an ordinary way. What happens when the switch flips is not that you found a door out of the box. It's that you feel yourself being out there. With something of a shock, you recognize this perspective is familiar; in fact, you've been out there right along. You can hear the little self you *thought* you were rattling around inside the box, trying really hard.

"So how do I . . . " The question just will never stop. It isn't about getting from here to there. This is why time doesn't matter. Why time won't help. The thing is *already* the case. All that changes is you go from not realizing it to realizing it.

If you are inclined toward prayer, then pray every single moment to be shown yourself. If you aren't inclined toward prayer, then lift *seeing* – seeing this that you are – to the top of any possible pile that might otherwise absorb your attention (like all the stuff inside the box).

When you pray, you aren't asking a god for help. Or a spirit of any sort. It might look that way. It might create a kind of container, a perceived route, to think of a prayer going somewhere, toward something, toward someone with the power to grant a blessing.

But what prayer really is, stripped down, is a way of inviting what's knowable to be known. Allowing recognition. It is the case, after all, that the only reason this isn't universally seen is that the eyes aren't open. Which is why trying to get yourself to go in a certain direction, thinking there is a secret route out, formulating the right kind of question, will never reveal anything.

Once you see, you cannot un-see. Looking for this in the usual way constantly amounts to using your eyes to look outside yourself. To look for something elsewhere, someplace to go, to discover. When all the while, the viscous jellies in your skull, if they could only be allowed to, would sense themselves, their own perfection.

It's like that. It's like trying to see the top of your own head, or trying to see your eyelids or your teeth. *Feel yourself.* Sense that you are here. That you are able to sense. What is it that is capable of sensing itself? When something is known, what is doing the knowing?

It's going on the entire time the attention is elsewhere. It's why stillness is conducive. When you get very still, when you stop looking, or trying, something can feel itself. In that feeling, there are no questions. There is nobody there, not the usual sort of somebody anyhow. Yet *awareness* is. Awareness has nothing to do with anything inside the box. But it can see the box, clear as day.

The stuff inside the box was put there by your mind.
Every blessed scrap of it.

The Ultimate Betrayal

We are betrayed daily, hourly, by the persisting sense of self. That sense of *who I am*, and how it tends itself, how it keeps itself seeming real. It's a betrayal because of how it keeps us from noticing the spaciousness around the self, around everything – the container, you might say. The space around and within all that ordinarily holds our attention. The delicious stillness that cannot be ruined, or in any way altered.

It's only for the pretty constant absorption in the real-seeming self that we miss the *felt* experience of the more real thing. It isn't, of course, a "thing" (there is no good word for it). But we can say with certainty that it's real. And that it is palpable. Feel-able.

We can observe that in the moments it's felt, the usual sense of self is absent.

Which is telling. That the two – the spaciousness and the self – are not experienced simultaneously. Each is a world, you might say, unto itself. More to the point, for anyone seeking the peace that passeth understanding, is this: the familiar self (the very one doing the seeking) is not capable of attaining the longed-for stillness. The reason the stillness is felt, when it is, is that the self has fallen apart. Its maintenance crew has dispersed. Which is to say, thought has stopped.

So the task, for one who wants this, is first to see that the one doing the wanting is incapable of getting. To realize that there is no thought, no succession of thoughts, that can get you to the place *beyond* thought. And then to omit no opportunity to observe, without judgment or any attempt to change anything, how that real-seeming self keeps itself going. To recognize the maintenance crew every time it shows up. To understand that *this* – self-maintenance – is what is going on.

Any attempt to improve that self, in the name of attaining the longed-for well-being, is a colossal waste of effort. That self is the very thing that's in the way. Trying to fix the self – to enlighten it – is like scoring points for the other side. You are already in the end zone, your arms around the precious thing, but then you turn and run the length of the field to the *wrong* end zone, all the while carrying the impression of "making progress." This is many people's idea of the spiritual life, working so hard to bring the terminally limited self to perfection, when *perfection* was already right where they were, and all they're doing is distancing themselves from it by continuing to fuss over what might as well be a doll, an action figure.

If only they would have held still and looked around – not with the eyes of the unperfectible self, but with the awareness that is not subject to conditioning, to dissatisfaction, to wishing things were otherwise than they are.

This awareness – the knower of the peace that passeth understanding – has no opinions, no habits, no beliefs, no cherished or lamented history. It does not compare itself with how it wishes it would be. It bears no grudges, is identified with nothing, would not think to object to anything or try to manipulate it to match some image of the desirable. It does not exert effort. It has never felt afraid or proud or ambitious. It does not experience time. Thought does not feel real to it.

So . . . *by definition* . . . anything in you that DOES do those things is calling attention to itself as being unreal and not worth indulging. Certainly not worth imagining that such a self could attain perfection. Best to give yourself a break from all that. Instead, ask yourself – all day long – *What am I? What's real?* See if you can notice how it's possible, *always,* when you hold still (even in the middle of the most god-awful fray), to sense awareness itself. *To tell that you exist.* You can feel yourself being. And you don't have to resort to thought in order to bring this about.

Meanwhile, each time one of those expressions of the familiar, limited self shows up, instead of entering into it, trying to answer its silly questions, to pursue what it thinks is important, instead of all that, do this: notice how these are the ways it maintains itself, by dignifying all of that wasted effort.

And then step to the side of it and look around you. Notice what your senses are picking up. Feel your bodily sensations (including anything emotional that's grinding around inside, *without getting sucked back into the thought stream).* See if you can feel what awareness itself feels like, how free it is of thinking. Notice how it feels different from the way thinking feels.

The awareness capable of this natural observation is the spaciousness. It is incapable of betrayal.

There's a rivalry between living and thinking. Between time and the now. But it's a rivalry that's underground, unseen. Never examined, even as it's felt to be crazy-making. The strain is palpable. This rivalry is the primary atmosphere of our lives, the background music. The underlying, persistent tension between wanting not to have missed actual life, the sumptuous thing itself – *felt* experience, with you engaged, really here for it, as it's delivered into your welcoming hands – between that and the mind's idea of what life might yet be, or should have been. Could have been.

It's a tug of war, the two competing for the affections and attention of one person. Live or fret? Savor or process? Relax into reality or feel sorry for yourself, ball up your fists, as if life were the enemy.

Time isn't precious. Time is a thought about before or later. It's the moment that's precious. This one. Not the slew of them on the horizon. What makes you think that when you get there, to the longed-for future, it will suddenly be possible to be in the present – more possible than it is right now?

It's not what you *think* about the moment that's precious, because as soon as the thinking starts up, your attention is no longer *here*. It's shifted to the content of the thought, as if *that* were the now.

The love of the possible future is all about content. As if what you do in, or with, the now is what makes it worth living. Precious.

Alas. The focus on the content means the *container* is missed. Consciousness being the container. The content, actually, is irrelevant. What a revelation. Just before death, the truth of this becomes vivid. Let it become vivid now. Don't waste the rest of your life lying to yourself about the transformational value of content.

The rivalry is between living and avoiding living. Are we afraid to live? Afraid, maybe, of getting it wrong?

But the moments fly by, and soon enough the curtain falls.

What are you waiting for?

The End of the Story

For the longest time there is the story, the one you equate with reality. You don't see it as a story, because you are its central character, not to mention author. For the longest time it's like this, and then something causes you to see it as a story.

The story has compelled you. Probably it still does, long after you've seen it's a story. It has twisted you into knots. Sometimes you feel located outside of it and are able to be aware of yourself reacting and investing in a way you weren't before. You watch and you learn. You see the ways you keep it all going.

You get good at knowing it isn't what you are, at least intellectually. But then the time for that comes to an end. It needs to come to an end. When you truly stop investing in the story, it falls apart. If you keep indulging it, ministering to the earnest protagonist, declaring it all "just a story," you are giving it a kind of attention, endowing it with a degree of reality and importance that keeps it going. You are filling its tank with premium fuel, and then wondering why it never stops.

The whole point is to stop living parallel lives. To let the story completely undo itself, and then find out what it feels like to be alive.

When you get that the person in the story is not who or what you really are, you turn your back on it and walk away. Right off a cliff, maybe, but you leave it behind.

It will never let *you* go. If you are waiting for it to lose interest in itself, you will wait forever.

If you're not ready to walk away, then turn back toward the story and step right back into it with a whole heart, forgetting you ever saw it from that distance. Because it was a forced distance, a mental distance, an artificial point of view adopted by some kind of spiritual orientation. If you still think there's something to heal from, stay there. You're not ready to be done with it.

Once you've seen the falsity, it cannot hold together anymore.

The irony of it. The thing you seek is whole and has never been otherwise. That which needs healing is a cardboard figure of a life. But as long as you experience it as having heat and blood and hunger, then – from that point of view – it appears as though healing is essential.

You can't do both at once – turn your back on it and lovingly attend it. You either are or are not the story. If you still feel drawn to tending it (recovering, understanding root causes of your issues, generating new chapters), don't tell yourself you can simultaneously step out of it.

None of this can be forced or prematurely accomplished. Readiness is all. You are or you aren't ready. Just don't kid yourself meanwhile that you can go in both directions at once. All you'll accomplish is nothing at all. At the worst, create the illusion you've gotten somewhere, when you haven't. Be in a pretty regular state of self-lying.

It's like finding out the truth about Santa Claus. Once there is even the tiniest crack in the story (like when it dawns on you that reindeer can't actually fly) – once you realize your personness has substance *only when you THINK it into being* – there is structural damage to the self with continuity and importance and separation. It all just shatters. It cannot hold itself together anymore.

Until then, it's just a lot of stories you're telling yourself about how you know it's all just a story, and you the main character. About how you know you aren't your beliefs or your unfortunate conditioning. Your present-tense issues. You *do* think you're all of that. You even *like* being all of that, in the way a pig revels in the mud. You've just heard that you're not "supposed to" define yourself by the drama, not according to the books you've read and the things that get said. Learning how to say the right things. The lingo. Just more ways to stay in the dark but to have the illusion of progress.

It might be good, even restful, to reconsider what you're after. Nothing in the world wrong with having just a regular life. Reveling in the story. Why not? It's not so bad. Sometimes it's even a blast. Poignant too. Certainly poignant.

Or get on with it. If you want to get on with it, just do it. Time's a-wastin'.

Getting It in Your Head Versus Getting It in Your Bones

When a radical insight comes, so startling is the perspective shift that it appears to have occurred entirely out of the blue. More likely, it's the culmination of a process that's been under way for some time, perhaps unobserved.

When it deeply dawns that you are not your thoughts – when that reality penetrates consciousness, like sunlight suffusing the horizon – the solidity of thought has probably been chipping away for some time. The dissolution of the self has been quietly taking place. Around the edges of awareness, now and again you've intuited the artificiality and randomness of mental activity. There've been moments of seeing that you actually *decide* to believe what you do. The outline of a story has been seen, its content less substantial and compelling. The paltry consolation of an inner narrative has been realized, and turned from, in favor of the unmediated encounter with reality.

In those "before" times (the ones preparing you for the ultimate revelation), it happens something like this. From habit, a story starts spinning itself. Then the utter invention of it comes into view. Awareness takes hold of the dangling thread, pulling loose all the stitches of the half-made thing, leaving you briefly at peace, in the presence of reality (rather than in the presence of your thoughts). But then life goes on. Soon enough the pattern starts up again, and very likely you buy into the reality of the next story, wrapping yourself in its false comfort. (Maybe you are dimly aware of this taking place, but it feels so good that you avert your eyes from the truth, from the thinness of the mental invention.)

Until the radical dawning, thought will continue to compel. Until it no longer can.

Only when you're equipped to see will you see: your entire life you've mistaken the contents of your mind for *you*. Only then will you directly experience the authentic vitality, the *something* that can feel itself *be*, utterly independent of memory, belief, consolation. You will know *that* is what you are.

It's a shock to the system. The thing suddenly seen, suddenly obvious. How can it have not been obvious before?

You can't get a thing until you are ready to get it. Thinking about it a little harder won't get you there. Long before you feel it in your viscera, you "got it" in your head. You could repeat the neat formulation *(My thoughts are not reality)*. But you kept on generating thoughts and believing them, as if they were a piece of free-standing reality. You kept suffering.

Until the truth enters your bones like a warm morning, you can *think* about it all day, telling yourself you know you're not your thoughts. Your mind understands plenty, which is as close to really getting it as a pencil sketch of a peach approximates warm juice in the mouth.

Until your mouth is brimming with juice, don't waste your time trying to talk yourself into anything. Meanwhile, do not avert your eyes. When you see you're buying into a self-made story, for God's sake *stop*. Let the stitches unravel. Unclothed in the mind's comforting inventions, you are more available to the sun.

An Encyclopedia of a Peach

There appears to be a *you* having an objective existence, independent of your mind's narrative of a self. The further impression is that this *you* has experiences. The you looks like a noun (changeable but roughly stable), while the experiences are like verbs and adjectives. (Something's *happening* to you or by you, and it's good or bad.) Supporting the impression of an objectively-occurring you is the physical body. Yet it's easy to see there's a great deal more to "you" than your body (bones, blood, electrical impulses, liver, brain).

If you're inclined to spiritual inquiry, or susceptible to impressions of varying "levels" of reality, it may appear as though the objectively-existing you has, broadly speaking, two categories of experience. One is the ordinary (having meaning to the ego-mind), and the other is the *extra*-ordinary. There will, of course, be a preference for the latter.

The extraordinary is marked by a pronounced relief from the familiar strain and limitation. Time seems to have stopped. A sense of well-being pervades. The mind is quiet. What have appeared to be problems no longer stand out in the landscape, or carry any emotional weight. The enduring impression of separation has settled like sand in water. "You" don't seem to be there at all.

Yet there is awareness. If you are a truth-seeker, or just weary of regular life, and there's a memory of the exquisite peace outside the limitations of ordinary mental processing, you may yearn for more of that. You cherish the recollection of what it was like, fondling the memory like a jewel in your pocket.

Pursuit of another one of *those* (or better yet, a sustained "condition") may become your primary focus.

* * * * *

The appearance of an objectively-existing *you* capable of having two kinds of experience is flawed at the start. The illusory nature of this real-seeming you is where the focus should go, rather than on seeking the preferred type of experience. You (as you ordinarily understand yourself to be) are capable of only one kind of experience: the kind the ego can have.

Here's what happens. The mind thinks up a *you,* which appears to have an objective reality, and then that *you* has experiences. What's obvious is the part about having experiences. It's the first part that gets neglected: that your very *self* is created by the mind, assembled from mentally-produced material such as memory, label, identity, belief. In reality, there *is* no objectively-occurring you, independent of thinking it into being. There is only *this moment,* as lived (sensed, moved, felt) by the momentary form "you" are taking. Everything else is mind-generated: story, idea, emotional burden and its physical residue. If all of your mind's content were wiped out, but you were still aware and alert, your brain undamaged, your experience would be reduced to the sensing of the immediate scene and the sensation in your body. You would not know the name for anything (yourself included), nor would you have any conceptual framework for anything you perceived. There would be no interpretation, no meaning-giving. Just awareness, observation, sensation. Direct encounter, without any intervening mental filters. Since your mind would have no prior content to make reference to, you would have – you would *be* – only *this,* right here. Knowing would be direct. Original. Utterly fresh. Like the awareness of an animal, an infant. You would be curious. Fearless.

* * * * *

The awareness that "experiences" the extraordinary is an intelligent spaciousness lacking personal features. It does not seek a certain kind of experience. Let alone does it judge, resist, or attach meaning. The mind-made you cannot do anything *but* interpret, seek, prefer, be dissatisfied. Being the center of its own universe, it has its eye on self-preservation. Its vigilance is unrelenting. The two – spacious intelligence and the mind-made self – have nothing whatever to do with one another. One does not touch the other. What each kind of awareness experiences as reality is unavailable to the other. The ego-mind has no access to anything outside itself. Awareness can't be bothered with the ego's idea of reality.

The ego-mind can experience only itself and its creations (opinions, emotions, identities). It cannot look beyond itself. It is incapable of seeing anything – itself included – without the bias of its own filters. It is incapable of awakening, of escaping its own gravitational pull.

* * * * *

If you stood in a town square and stopped passersby to ask how many kinds of experience they've had, they'd say "too many to count." Certainly not just *one*. At the very least, there are the good experiences and the bad ones. Or the significant ones and the unmemorable ones. Each broad category contains numerous sub-sets: the good experiences having to do with love, with work, with creativity. Then there are the good love experiences that *lasted* and those that didn't. And so on, endlessly refinable. Millions of verbs and adjectives. The point of view *here*, however, puts all ordinary experience into a single category, as distinct from the extra-ordinary. The feature *shared* by all ordinary experiences – from the euphoric to the devastating – is vastly more significant than their apparently valuable distinctions. What they share is that they are experienced by the mind-made self. They are, in fact, *created* by it. Once the lived momentary reality has been incorporated by the ego-mind (which occurs with lightning speed), the "reformatted" reality is all you've got of whatever actually happened. What would life be like if that process *didn't* occur? What would it feel like to be "you"?

* * * * *

During a moment of extraordinary awareness, you may notice that the familiar you is nowhere to be found. That conspicuous absence has everything to do with the exquisite nature of the moment.

You may be saying, *If I'm not there at such a moment, how is noticing possible?* Awareness is there. It's capable of noticing. It's just that it has no agenda.

But then, if you ask yourself what sort of intelligence asked that question about how noticing can happen, you will see it's the ordinary mind.

* * * * *

If the you that you appear to be has no objective existence, why does it feel so real, so enduring? Subject to threat, requiring of vigilant attention? The evolving human mind became incredibly skillful at symbolic representation of reality. Language and the ability to visualize mean the mind's illustrated story of outer life seems as real as reality itself. (In fact, the mental rendering tends to *eclipse* reality entirely, because it's mistaken for reality.) This capacity has served us on a practical level, enabling our species to survive physical threats, adapt to the conditions of our environment, and create civilizations. In our early evolution, our mental picture-stories of threat related to the risk of starvation or predator attack – challenges to our physical existence. The trouble is that we tend to extend the mind's gifts – to misapply them, as it turns out – to the creation of a self, which appears (like so many thoughts) to have an objective reality. When that self experiences threat (rejection, challenge to identity, instability), it's felt to be an *existential* threat, because we have come to equate the ego-mind (along with the body) with "who we really are." A serious challenge to the seeming reality of the mind's sense of self is felt with the same emotional intensity as if it were a tiger bearing down. Meanwhile, the *you* experiencing danger isn't even what you most deeply are. But because the self that's subject to threat demands such vigilance, the Other is forgotten. It is, after all, so quiet and unmoving. It's spaciousness itself, without agenda.

* * * * *

The only "you" that is real, actual, *lived* – that isn't filtered through the mind – is the sensed encounter with momentary reality. That is all. The now is all you will ever have of life. Of yourself. It is all you've ever actually experienced. Every memory, every scrap of conditioning, was born as a *now*. See the difference between what is sense-able and feel-able, and what can be understood, named, narrated, recalled.

When the mind is still, there is no space between "you" and the now. Life is direct encounter.

Only, there is no separate encounter-ER. There's no one being immersed "in" the moment. The moment *is* what you are, right then.

And that is all. That is all "you" are, ever: momentary reality as experienced in a feeling and intelligent body.

Yes, really. Everything else is a collection of memories held in the mind, as if in a suitcase, which is lugged into and out of every adventure.

We mistake ourselves for the contents of the suitcase. It's the difference between a set of encyclopedias about a peach . . . and a peach.

The now is born and it dies, with the speed of a breath. If you aren't in your head, "you" are there for reality, sensing and feeling. In the aftermath (the next *now)*, there is memory of that moment, and whatever the mind wants to make of it, as well as any emotion that might be stirred by the thought. But that recollected and processed "now" no longer has an objective reality. It "exists" in the mind only.

Just as you do. The *you* that you believe yourself to be has no independent reality. It's produced and maintained by your processing mind, which is serving (almost constantly) at the pleasure of the ego, which has you convinced that it's *you.*

What you really are is fleeting, ever-changing. Thrillingly *here,* alive. If only you knew it.

It's only when the mind-self turns on, with its assessing and story-making, that the familiar you assembles. Awareness becomes distant from what-is. You are no longer living in life; you are living in your head.

Many people spend their entire lives in their heads. When it comes time to die, they feel as though they haven't lived. They're right.

The awareness that knows itself in the now is not the you that lives in the head.

The you that the mind thinks up is incapable of experiencing the extraordinary peace and well-being of the no-you state. Even to call it a state is imperfect. None of the language here can ever be anything but a wooden approximation (language, a mental tool, being at a distance from reality).

* * * * *

To the ordinary you, this picture of reality, of self, is likely to be disturbing. At the very least, disappointing. Possibly truly alarming.

But! In those moments of transcendent awareness, the one capable of alarm is not in evidence.

Only if it were *there* could it be troubled by its absence.

The fact that the familiar you is missing from those extraordinary moments is a crucial piece of data. Disregard it and you will continue moving in useless loops, seeking the preferred kind of experience.

It's only to the mind-made self that there appears to be a locked door separating "you" from the spaciousness that is your fundamental nature.

Trying to get the ego to experience transcendence is as worthwhile as searching for a key to a door that has no lock.

The Power of Attention

The less you experience your separateness, the appearance of a defined self, the more readily consciousness pours anywhere attention goes. It comes with the territory. The less defended you are, the less attached to an identity, or to your own history or longings, the more you experience directly what's going on "out there." Because it is no longer *other*.

This is why there is no effort to be compassionate, no remembering-to-be-kind required. No need to extend beyond your insular concerns to care for another, to wish a stranger well. That *is* "you" over there. All has become self-interest.

But what does this mean, when everywhere you look there is suffering? Are you therefore bound to suffer because there is violence and fear everywhere there is human life? Does it all become "your" suffering?

How is it possible to exist in a condition of peace in this unpeaceful world?

Not long ago there was the news of a man going after his young children with a hatchet, shortly before setting off the conflagration that silenced them all, and what happened to awareness in the encounter with that news? The feeling was of *me* doing that, with that hatchet, that gasoline poured all around. Me being the confused and terrified child. Each experience of *being that,* of my heart breaking, lasted maybe a few seconds. Awareness touched, entered, then withdrew.

The media call the man a monster, and I understand what that's about. But that is so far after the primary thing: *This is what we humans do.* Can do. Are subject to.

We are all the same, all one thing. It pleases us to declare ourselves different, better. That belief assists our impression of sanity, of morality.

Another thing. Trivial, by comparison. But trivial only in the realm of idea, not in actual experience. And in the same way as the nightmare of father-with-children, illustrative of what happens when the accustomed boundaries between self and other are no longer experienced as reality. My cat got hold of a chipmunk. During the brief interval in which I intervened, trying to assess the presence or absence of vitality in the stripy body, looking into the glazed black eyes, I *was* the chipmunk. If I had lingered there, I would have kept hurting. Unnecessarily.

When I looked into the green eyes of the cat, I felt the visceral rush of predation.

Here's the thing. Attention is free to go where it wants. It can stay with the chipmunk or with the father swinging the hatchet, or it can stay with the people in a car accident I recently rolled past. It can stay with the people near the Fukushima power plant, or the people crumbling with the World Trade towers, or the polar bears with no solid place to climb onto. Attention *could* stay these places, or inside the heart of my terribly depressed child.

It can also decline to.

This could be pronounced denial. There is such a thing as denial, distracting self from what brings pain. Pushing away the uncomfortable feelings in the presence of reality, taking refuge in some kind of comforting thought that pushes like a wall against feeling. With denial, a person is absolutely separate, absolutely other. Not experiencing what's happening over there (or even right here, within, because we force this same distance within ourselves).

This is not that.

Once the sense of separateness has dissolved, every conscious moment you are vaguely but truly aware of being, literally *being,* all that is. This is the truth of what we are. When the awareness is of that, there is an inborn and steady sense of freedom, deliberateness, about where within all-that-is to put attention. Which includes where to decline to put it. Attention is like light. You aim it, and there you see. But you never lose the larger background awareness. Like liquid, light fills all the space.

When attention allows itself to be on space itself, the space in which all occurs – on no particular something within the space – there is no impression of someone "doing" it. No breaking heart. Just awareness sensing itself.

But we are people. Apparently particular, physical. Located in a point in space. Moving, assuming roles, loving, building. Being sick, aging. Alive, for a time. And all the while this larger awareness flooding whatever occurs, with its quality of deliberateness, the freedom to allow attention to go one place to the exclusion of others, in a given moment. The absolute freedom to withhold it.

Such is the experience of formlessness expressing itself through human form. There is no contradiction, no inconsistency. Incarnation stretches the mind's ability to understand.

To formlessness, suffering has no meaning. It's just . . . molecules, energy, flux, doing and undoing. Phenomena. But as soon as awareness resumes its humanness, assuming the necessary particularity, you have to figure out what to do with attention. You *could* spend life hanging on a crucifix, because there is violence and fear everywhere you look. You could do that, let your heart break ceaselessly every day of your conscious life. But only if you choose to.

Yes, the heart broke for the father swinging the hatchet. Imagine his agony, to be brought to such a thing. He was not born a monster.

What Awakeness Feels Like

What is the feeling quality of awakeness? When it's sustained, the norm, the default, what does it feel like? Some describe it as exquisite tenderness, as universal and unconditional love. People often have the impression that the awake "state" is rapturous, an intensely joyful high without end. Some say it is without any texture at all, that the absence of egoic emotion means the awake state is neutral, empty of anything recognizable as feeling.

This gets talked about, even debated, often in a very heady way, among those attempting to understand. It gets explored by those meaning to clear the air of cobwebs, to get the rose color out of the lenses, as regards what wakefulness is like.

There is a lot of confusion about this. For one thing, someone looking at it from the outside – someone thinking about it, wondering – is stuck with looking at an *idea* about it, which will never yield anything but more ideas. Someone who is "in" it, who *is* it, looking with its own eyes at itself and trying to describe it, must resort to words, which depend on ideas and images for their meaning.

But we don't seem to be able to stop trying to convey it; the wondering what-it's-like continues. So here I go, giving it a shot.

First, to make one thing clear: whatever feeling there may be – of joy, of tenderness, peaceful well-being – it is not the same as what's experienced in ordinary human-heart experience, where an emotion has its opposite, a cause, and a lifespan, and is felt to be personal. It is subject to change, to watering-down, dissolution, poisoning. When people speak of the feeling state of awakeness, of the absence of familiar human emotion, this is what they are calling attention to – the absence of the familiar stuff of life on the roller coaster. Nor is it the ordinary human experience of joy turned high, as is often imagined. Yet what else can a person do but imagine that – start with what is known, familiar, and magnify the idea of that?

It is the case, even so, that when someone's mind first goes utterly quiet, and the machinery of suffering has disassembled itself, there may be the experience of intense joy. This comes of the radical contrast with how it always was before, from the felt contrast between that and This. The stunned revelation that you are not what you thought you were, and the relieving of self-caused misery, can leave you feeling quite ecstatic . . . for a time. But then you come to feel a kind of normal, baseline ease. You've gotten used to not hitting yourself in the head with a hammer, and you forget to notice how good it feels, because the old way is a distant memory.

In the search for an adequate image for awakeness, the closest I can come is space. At its most expansive expression in a human being (as far as "I" have felt, anyhow), awakeness feels like space itself. In that space, anything can (and does) occur. Within it, life happens, with all its variety and energy and motion. But the space itself has no experience, no feeling, no movement or noticeable quality, apart from a subtle "self"-awareness – the space sensing itself. Whatever occurs in the space is experienced as mere phenomena. The profound neutrality of this spacious awareness can look like heartlessness.

The morning the jets plowed into the World Trade Center, there was hideous suffering, which those of us not in one of the jets or in one of the towers, or in the vicinity, or loving someone in a tower or a jet, are not able to imagine, however much we may have unwittingly tried.

But the space around the tall buildings, and inside them, and the space between the running people, and the space between the atoms of the bodies of those crushed and burning and dying – the space that surrounded each thing, each agony, the space that penetrated the pieces of burning paper, that came between two thoughts of a person about to pass out of consciousness forever, the space between one floor and another as the top one collapsed onto the lower one (have you had enough?) – the space *did not care*, did not know or ask about suffering, about meaning. The morning sky, though it filled with ash and fume, though its color briefly changed, did not care, was not permanently altered. It stood in plain, radically unfeeling recognition of the unfolding disaster, which had no meaning whatever.

This space, this spaciousness, is the experience of awakeness in its most depersonalized expression, well beyond the sense of being a person, or an anything.

This is not a comfortable or comforting thought, especially to one who wants to wake up because of the expectation of unending bliss.

But what about that exquisite tenderness, the unconditional love? The profound compassion that naturally flowers, as you realize that all human beings suffer (as you once did) unnecessarily? What about the ecstasy that (yes) visits you on occasion, so intense it almost hurts? What of the mystical union with the divine? Doesn't something of these experiences also occur?

In order to function in a normal human life – to
engage in relationships, have a job, make a meal, have
fun, participate in political or social or creative
activities – awakeness assumes form, the form of a
human being. The human being has a body, a history,
a name, a personality, looks a certain way, lives in a
certain place, does particular kinds of things, interacts
with other human beings. Although it readily adopts
all of this (in most awakened lives, anyhow), it doesn't
get confused, in that old familiar way, and start
believing any of it is ultimate reality. Awakeness
doesn't identify with any of it or get attached
particularly. Nevertheless, it participates. At this
"level," there is abundant feeling. Here is where
tenderness lives, where compassion is felt, where fun
can be had. In this expression of awakeness that is
closer to earthly life than the profoundly neutral
space, here is where unconditional love feels itself
everywhere attention goes. It is where sensation
occurs. Where pain is experienced – not the needless
mind-caused suffering of before, but the authentic
alive pain that comes with, say, grief over the death of
a loved one. (And it is not resisted, so it doesn't
cripple, or endure forever.) Physical pain also occurs,
and is not resisted or otherwise mentally managed.

It may be useful to contemplate the incarnation in this
connection. The difference between the formless and
the embodied is the difference between featureless
space and the ability to savor, revel, care for. It isn't a
one-or-the-other thing. Christ was a person, and he
also realized he wasn't only a person. Sometimes he
appeared heartless. And he wanted only to relieve
others of their suffering.

Pausing the River

Something not seen or understandable has its way with you. Something says *okay, that part is done, and now it's time for something else to happen.* Quietly disassembles the house, taking apart the joints, silent tools at work, screws backing themselves out of their threaded holes.

You don't even notice it happening. It's just that all of a sudden there is light where before there was a structure. Air moving, and you feel it. There is recognition of something having been removed. Now what? But no need to ask, because it's already here, apparent.

The sensation is of utter passivity. Receptivity. No muscle tension, no reaching. Not even waiting, because it's already under way. Whatever the heck it is. Not trying to know what it is. It doesn't care to have a name for itself, a map with coordinates. But clearly "you" aren't doing it, whatever it is. This much is clear.

It's like waking up and discovering you're on a ride, a carnival that's been under way for a while, having started sometime before now, and the only thing that's changed, on waking, is that now you're aware of it, whereas before you weren't. Awareness wasn't. Once awareness is, if the feet can manage to resist feeling around for brakes, and the hands rest in the lap instead of trying to curl themselves to a phantom steering wheel . . . more will happen. Even if the hands think they've found a wheel, they find it just spins round and round, because it has no connection to the momentum and direction things seem to be taking.

An ancient philosopher wrote about life as a river, stepped into once. The river just goes. The onrushing bank that isn't there, but the industrious mind invents an image of one. As if it were possible to get to shore and climb out. To pause the river. Awareness isn't one thing and life the other. A person cannot "be" aware, as if the person and awareness were discrete. Awareness cannot feel itself be except in the rushing water.

Find yourself without awareness. Keep being without being aware. Go ahead and try.

The grasping for an onrushing rock, a mossy clump of shore, someplace to climb out onto, sit and dry off. It's like reaching your hand into a 3D image. It sure looks real. The hand keeps being genuinely surprised to come up with nothing solid. The only solid thing is the hand.

When the hand stays at rest, the image of the shore takes itself apart. The silent little tools disassembling things. You aren't "in" the river. There isn't anything *but* a river. And it has no banks.

The impression keeps forming itself that you are in a river, and the river has banks.

Awareness turns itself on. Life has begun. When awareness feels itself, so long as the mind isn't moving in with its noisy hammers and power drills and circular saws, filling the air with sawdust (oh, but look here! not only is there a shore, there are *houses* on the shore!) – as long as that which is merely aware is left the space to sense itself – the search is over. There is not even a memory of having been searching.

The water wouldn't think to look for itself. Does it feel itself moving? Movement makes no sense unless there is something that isn't moving. On a train beside another train, looking out the window, you sense one of them moves. There is no knowing which. Or caring. You can't see the track, or the sky. Awareness is on a train. There might be a track down there, but you just will never see it.

Awareness *is* a train. There is nobody on the train.

When the silence comes, when life turns itself off, the train disappears. As long as you are able to notice that you be, it's happening. On a train, there is the sensation of being at rest, so long as you don't assemble a self, get up, and try to move in a way that's counter to the movement of the train. Like, trying to go faster in the same direction, or walking toward the back of the car. Inevitably, you stumble.

Human Being as Lint

A woman reached out awhile ago and asked if we might connect. She was at the end of her rope. Depressed for decades, she had tried, as far as she knew, every possible thing.

Her affect was flat. I had only her voice, not her facial expressions or body posture, our times together being via telephone. I remember vividly the first time I heard her laugh, after a few sessions. How tears came to my eyes. I hadn't known what her laugh might sound like, or if I'd ever get to find out.

Sometimes she falls silent for a long while. Then, when she says something after that silence, I know where she is, even if I don't focus on the content of her words. I can *feel* her. It's the texture of her voice. There is such tenderness. Awe. It's come about from some deep recognition. There is such gratitude, the recognition that something very big is going on.

What changed was that she came to see the beliefs she'd imprisoned herself in. Not to judge them, or herself for having them; not to replace them with different ("better") beliefs, or to struggle to sort out whether they were "true." But just to see that they were there, and how profoundly they had boxed her in. And that *she* had brought them into being.

She saw her beliefs had no independent existence, beyond the walls of her cranium. Things like what it means to be a good mother. Like what she deserves, and does not deserve. On and on. Once the door opened a crack, the revelation came in a flood. The overarching insight: how powerful beliefs are, how imprisoning. And that we are their makers.

There was nothing unavailable to that light. Nothing she would look away from. Of course she laughed! The absurdity of it all.

She didn't have to talk herself out of the beliefs, but simply to see that they were there. To recognize when one was in motion.

She doesn't, like many people who long to stop suffering, pick and choose what she is willing to see. She is utterly unafraid. She wants the truth, at all costs. She wants the bottom line. So she does not recoil. She is curious, wide-eyed, entirely available to the inner light.

Sometimes she's bubbling over to say what's been happening since our last conversation. Not the story of her life but what's been happening inside: what she's seen, what she's struggled with, what's fallen away. She is not lazy. No grass grows under her feet.

She is a lover of the truth. This is different from being a lover of safety, of comfort. You see, in the face of wanting to know, everything falls. There are no sacred cows, no closets too dark to flood with light.

She said once that she was shocked to realize how *every single piece of what she thinks of as her "self"* is something that's been stuck on. Every significant experience, every belief, every identity, every story she tells herself, every agony, every desire, every fear – she saw, with blinding clarity, that all of it has clung to her, defined her, made itself into something heavy to carry through her travels. And that it all exists in the mind. Every scrap of it.

"It's like lint stuck to me! A million bits of lint." She laughed – in joy. In relief.

The thing is, if you could somehow pick off all the lint . . . nothing would be left. It was only ever just stuck to itself. Like when you clean the lint trap in the dryer, and it all sticks to itself. It likes its own company. You can collect it into a compact ball and toss it. It's no big loss.

But what *is* a person without memory, belief, fear, longing? What is there if the mental filters of experience and hope are collected into a ball and discarded? Does a solid and continuous thing remain?

When your attention is riveted like a laser beam on something you've just discovered, or learned this very moment how to do, or when your eyes fall for the first time on a sequoia, or the face of your beloved, just returned from a long time away, what are "you" right then? When memory is not of interest, and there is nothing to want, or believe? When it's just awareness and the thing being reveled in, what are *you?*

See how "you" change, how insubstantial you are, when you experience yourself simply as a living moment. How in constant flux, constantly reforming, is this self. If you aren't ceaselessly telling yourself a story about what's happening, or about how things should be, but you're just living, now . . . what can be said to be you?

What if all your beliefs were put into the light, not assessed for their legitimacy, just seen as mental structures? Balled up like lint and allowed to blow away? What is it to purely encounter, to feel, to do, without slipping in a mental filter to look through, an intervening lens to enable interpretation, to tell you what to make of a thing, how to feel about it?

What if the story never even started up? Would it be restful? Ha! Would you laugh? A rollicking good time would be had. Such a relief.

Who is it that's laughing? When the lint is packed up, what's left? How is it possible to come to that essential thing, to the juice of existence itself, without ideas about it? Without all that jams up all the places the air and light would like to enter? How can you possibly know what's really going on if you rely on the inventions of the fearful mind to inform everything?

The cost of finding out is the willingness to ball yourself up in a great big useless collection of lint and let it float away. Your precious alleged self.

Something watches it float away. What *is* that something?

Transformative Suffering

There are two kinds of suffering: the kind that bears fruit, and the kind that's pointless (and therefore doomed to repeat).

Pointless suffering is the sort that occurs when – at a given moment – your entire sense of self is contained within the torture machine of mental and emotional anguish. All attention is on the current "problem" dished up by life, on the compelling appearance of the problem's objective reality. There's no consciousness in the picture, which (were it present) might enable you to step *outside* the turmoil and, from that more spacious perspective, observe the role of belief, your sense of identity, the tendency to story-making. To see how all of that – not the challenging piece of life – is actually what's brought about the misery.

Had it been enlivened in such a moment, consciousness might have transformed the present uproar into a teachable moment, giving you valuable insight into the role of the ego-mind in generating suffering. So you could stop blaming life for your self-inflicted misery. All of which would carry the potential to favorably affect subsequent episodes, very possibly relieving you of some considerable amount of angst. Hallelujah! Because to see the machinery operating, in real time in your own head and gut, is truly to learn, in a way all the books and teachers and retreats in the world can only point to, in a conceptual sort of way. Realizing you've stepped into the muck and then hanging out with the stuff on your shoes is another thing altogether. That kind of suffering bears fruit – provided you don't get bogged down in self-judgment.

For the greater part of humankind, pointless suffering is the only kind ever experienced. When life presents a challenge, the ego-mind takes over so completely that it's impossible to imagine there's anything more to awareness, right then, than the self-made definition of the problem. The dormant consciousness that's capable of *looking at* the whole thing is never roused. So the machinery of self-generated suffering runs smoothly and efficiently all of life, the person never suspecting their own part in causing it. Let alone that it could be otherwise. From one end of life to the other, they blame events they had no control over, their parents, genetics, the imperfect body, the economy, their ex. They die never realizing they needn't have experienced life the way they did (even with the outer circumstances unchanged).

For a small part of our species, higher consciousness blessedly is stirred enough to shine light on the anatomy of suffering, at least once in a while. There's a willingness to question the enduring assumption that *life* is to blame for the inner disquiet. There's a readiness to challenge the imprisoning belief that mental and emotional turmoil is an inevitable part of being human.

* * * * *

I am making a distinction here between mind-caused pain and the sort of pain having a physical cause, or one that comes of a loss like the death of a loved one. These latter kinds of pain are caused not by the mind but by a material fact that's directly felt. When mental filtering and story-making aren't resorted to, the surrender to "authentic" pain can be accompanied by a feeling of peace or radical aliveness – neither of which attends an episode of mind-made pain.

＊ ＊ ＊ ＊ ＊

A spiritual seeker is someone who's become curious about the nature of suffering, who is willing to reconsider some long-made assumptions. *Maybe I DO have a significant role in my ongoing angst, my inability to deeply rest. Maybe life could be a softer ride, by something changing within me.* A person looking at these possibilities has just entered that small and fortunate portion of humankind, for whom radical change in how life feels has become a vivid possibility.

So what happens then? The rising courage to confront one's inner trouble-maker brings about occasional moments of illumination. The familiar mental handling lets up a bit. There's the refreshing plain encounter with life itself, sans contraction, the filters of shoulds and shouldn'ts. There may be fleeting tastes of deep well-being and the quietly sweet sensation of aliveness.

But then . . . it happens again. Just about the time you thought maybe the monkey was off your back for keeps, something comes along that makes you realize it's got you again. In the face of a new life challenge, you go profoundly unconscious, ensnared in the familiar machinery of the mind and its emotion-making mess. Only an hour later (or a day, a week) do you realize how swamped you've been. *Sigh.* It can be discouraging, to say the least.

But take heart. Instead of aspiring to end all your misery (or to wake up already!), let your focus shift to *learning from suffering that occurs.* So it's not pointless. Remember: until you became a spiritual seeker, with the new orientation to your life and its alleged problems, all of your suffering was probably pointless. So when you're feeling frustrated about the fact that you still inflict pain on yourself, remember that. Now when you go into contraction, at least sometimes, you learn from it!

Being drawn into turmoil may actually be necessary – *if you're conscious of what's going on* – because maybe a person has to see, to suffer, the consequences of the mind's power to create an impression of reality. This seems to be the way we learn best. But if you put your attention on frustration and self-judgment, once you've become alert to a current bout of turmoil, you won't see what needs seeing. You won't discover what's generating the muck.

So don't look away, when you feel it happening again. Hang in there. Keep your eyes open. Back up and take the bigger view – the perspective that's available when you step back from all the emotion (including self-chastisement). You'll keep being granted these learning opportunities until you no longer need them. Might as well let them teach you.

And if you thought you'd learned already, look again. Look more deeply into the assumptions you don't even realize you've been making, having to do with what's true and right and inevitable. Once you *really* get what needs to be seen, it won't keep operating. It won't need to.

Preparing the Ground for Resistance

The pain caused by resisting is a pointless pain. So unnecessary. What if we were spared that? What a great blanket of misery would be lifted from life, which can be hard enough without that suffocating burden laid over it.

It's worthwhile to look at the anatomy of resistance. When somebody becomes aware of the option not to resist what is here, real, occurring . . . that awareness includes the recognition that resistance is *deliberately* (if unconsciously) done. When the light starts to come on, the choice unconsciously made is starting to become conscious. This is the radical discovery, no small thing: that what feels like an inevitable response (balking, denying, frustrated anger, etc., etc.) is actually not inevitable. The negativity we want to believe is inherent to the life development (as if there could be no other possible response) becomes subject to questioning. The radical opening is toward the insight that in fact option is at play.

When you discover that resistance is not inevitable, and you begin to explore the depth of suffering it engenders, then the other option comes alive. The matter of how acceptance opens the door to peaceful well-being – regardless of what life is dishing out – becomes increasingly vivid.

The question of whether or not the preferred thing has taken place becomes blessedly irrelevant, in terms of the condition of your inner state.

But there's more, a lot more, and this *more* is worth exploring in your own experience.

After the discovery of choice has come alive for a person accustomed to knee-jerk resistance, what typically happens is that the reality of option will be viscerally felt, on some occasions, in the moment when the habitual resistance tries to start up. The engine begins to rev, and then you notice that creepy familiar feeling of tension in the body. You hear your mind muttering, and maybe your mouth. The fact that you are noticing these familiar patterns means a light has come on. You're noticing the pointless rigidity, feeling how it actually hurts. You're observing how you are, in effect, wrestling with reality, trying to get it to be different from what it is. You're seeing, maybe, the madness of the wasted effort.

Choice blossoms like a lotus. You reverse course, go soft, let unwind the terrible knot, the pushing-against. You say, quietly, *Yes, it is so.*

This is a two-step phenomenon. First you begin to resist. Then, because of the discomfort caused by resistance, the light comes on. You let go into reality, and rest comes. Two steps: push > surrender; tighten > relax.

But it may not be this way forever. You need the two steps only as a self-teaching device. Once the learning has occurred, you may wake up one day to realize there are no more two steps. That the habit of resistance, as the default, has unlearned itself. Acceptance has become the default. (Surely at this point you will have noticed that you are suffering much less than before.)

In a person to whom resistance doesn't occur at all, what is the state of mind, the condition in the body, that enables the environment of ongoing soft receptivity to reality? What is there, or what is missing, in such a person, that means resistance doesn't start up in the first place?

Here is the juicy part. We are moving toward exploring a deeper process, looking at a kind of suffering that (while more subtle) probably takes up more space, more weight and effort, than all the accumulated episodes of blunt resistance – the million times you've pitched a fit, groused, raged, obsessed over something that's occurred. This more subtle (but all-pervasive) suffering has to do with how people constantly prepare the ground for resistance. Take a look at the set-up that makes resisting well-nigh inevitable. And you don't even notice yourself doing it.

It's all got to do with assuming you know what's going to happen (or what's *not* going to happen). It's about expectation, about hope. About attachment to a particular outcome.

All of which, fundamentally, has to do with wanting to be in control. With predictability, the desire to know what's ahead (and what's not).

This is how the trap is set for inevitable resistance. It's why there's this current of anxiety running below so much of ordinary life, what accounts for the vigilance that attends our dealings, the radar alert to trouble, instability, danger. It's about the forward-moving momentum we fuel steadily, as if urging forward were necessary for anything to ever happen.

We don't like acknowledging the ongoingness of uncertainty, the vast force of chaos in which we live our lives. So we feed ourselves expectation, assumption, and hope. This is how we unconsciously set ourselves up to resist, later on. In order for things to change – for acceptance to become the comfortable norm – this prior trap-setting must become subject to conscious noticing. We constantly don't know what's around the corner, so we make ourselves tense (subtly or dramatically) with imagining that (say) the car will start, the plane will land, the house will stand, the job will hold, the milk won't spill, the bulb will stay illumined, the accident won't happen, the lover will remain loyal, the icy sidewalk won't cause a slip and a broken bone.

A person without expectation cannot be caught off-guard. Or startled. Or go into resistance. Resistance requires some prior assumption, or wish, that a certain thing will (or won't) happen. What if you are in an uninterrupted acknowledgment of not-knowing, not-controlling? It's not an acknowledgment that's mental. Though if the intelligent mind is consulted, it will see the truth of the radical and ongoing uncertainty that is the human condition. It will be unable to deny the brevity and changeability of every scrap of life.

But the deep recognition of not-knowing is a *visceral* thing, felt in the bone. When there is a beat of the heart, it is felt there, in the beat. It is experienced in the breath. Given this deep recognition, there will not be resistance, nor even the two-step sort of acceptance, starting with the initial impulse to push against.

Spiritual adept, beware: It doesn't work to start to resist and then (with your mind) to remind yourself that you aren't in control. The part where you hoped to be in control occurred long before the episode of resistance. What we're looking at here is how the ground was prepared for (well in advance of) the episode of resistance. This is a really good place to notice how spiritual knowledge can be misapplied (backwards!?!), how it can keep illusion going.

This isn't about becoming indifferent to outcome or ceasing to have preferences. It's about ceasing to be *attached* to your preference. It's about letting yourself deeply acknowledge how little control and predictability there is, and to stop grasping for the dream of these things.

Now, the strangeness is . . . Why does this absence of assumption, expectation, and hope amount to a *peaceful* condition, when it might look like a recipe for rampant fear?

Somewhere along the line, it has registered at an elemental level that your inner state needn't be subject to the balls pitched by life. That's one piece of it. Why fear life, or try fruitlessly to control it? But there's another thing, maybe more radical, or at least more surprising.

The truest heart of a human being is completely at home in the presence of the real (without regard for whether the real is "positive" or "negative"). When we are aligned with reality, without wishing it were different, without filtering it through a story (about meaning, good/bad, whatever), then *we are at peace*. Regardless of the circumstances. Being aligned with what-is is one way of understanding nonduality. You aren't separate from life. In order to resist, it's necessary first to (artificially) distance yourself from life. Hence the pain.

Something in us has known right along that we are not in control, the future being one big blank of the absence of what can be predicted or managed. The reality of the radical absence of control is something the deepest part of us aches to rest in. We've always known about the unpredictability, the limit on our power to shape what's ahead. The ego hates this, finding it extremely threatening, and works very hard to deny it, to wrest the illusion of control wherever it can be pitifully assembled via toothpicks and spit and tissue paper.

But see, if you don't consult the ego – if instead you let the bottom-level knowing rise up in your bones like warm water – you will become at last friendly with radical uncertainty, and will be able, finally, to radically rest. You'll be able to never again resist, or get caught off-guard; to never again anticipate or feel anxious or vigilant, or cling to a desired outcome.

Imagine the relief. How very lightly you will travel. No longer will life be your adversary.

What You Are (After You Disappear)

The sense of self dissolves, and how is it that what's left is radical cherishing? The cherishing is of all that is, and all-that-is has turned out to be what "you" actually are. So you are in the skin of the beloved, occupying the space defined by the presence of the beloved. Everywhere you go, everywhere you look, it is there.

This has been enabled by a disappearing act. You (who you thought you were) have become see-through. The muscles have untwisted; the grudges can't hold together any longer. The air moves right through you.

At night, I'm out there in the cold, black, still world with the old dog, who is melting a yellow pool of snow, and my eyes are drawn up. *Oh, hi!* Like I'd almost forgotten. The greeting to the firmament doesn't feel like it's reaching across vast distance. The stars seem to be saying hello to one another.

The strangeness is that although the cherishing has heat and vitality to it (being experienced in a living body), because there is no sense of a particular location or form of *what is being cherished*, it doesn't matter if dying occurs, or damage, or pain.

In ordinary commerce, if something is cherished, it's considered valuable. It's cared for, protected. The attachment is ferocious. But here, it's of no consequence if a piece of it goes away, because it's everywhere, always.

Because a human being has a mind, and is able to be self-reflective, we wonder at this odd coincidence of things. There is this cherishing going on – you could say, this *self*-cherishing – yet the prospect of demise is not distressing. Cherishing doesn't amount to a desperate effort to hold on to. Whatever happens is just what happens.

There is no more idea of that thing known as "my life." All there is is *this,* this that's happening now. It's all we ever know of life, of ourselves. Directly know, I mean. Feel, see, taste. All the rest – what constitutes "my life" – requires reference to the contents of the mind. It isn't real. It's a garbage can. Refuse, leftovers, anticipations. Stories. Oh, so many stories.

When subject and object lose their boundaries, when it's all one thing, one moment, that's life. And you are nowhere in it – not the you with stories and beliefs and fears – but the whole thing is what "you" sense yourself to be. It's all you know of life. Of course there is cherishing. Of course it is beloved. Even if it involves nausea and overdue bills. The whole measuring thing, the good versus the bad, has ceased to function. It doesn't occur to you to like or dislike. To like or dislike, it's necessary to first imagine that things could be other than they are, or to remember how they were before. It's necessary to experience self as separate from what-is. That function has been turned off. The mind is full of space. The reference points are gone.

The Moment the Lord Has Made

This is the day the Lord has made. Although I have read almost none of the Bible, these words often come spontaneously when I first step outside and greet the morning.

I wonder: did we make up the idea of God so joy would have a receptacle? The awe in the presence of what's here: what else to do with it but to ascribe it to an almighty generative force? What else to do with the rush of gratitude, on rising each morning, upon stepping out onto the porch and discovering that the blessed thing is still happening: the trees have stood all night, holding animals in their arms. The earth has held the trees' feet as I've slept.

Glory be to God for dappled things, said a poet priest, so in love with the physical world that he worried it made him profane.

I don't know if there is a god, but I want there to be. What else am I to do with what animates me, the surge up my bones on greeting the new day? How am I to possibly contain the tenderness of the thing I rest in when I lie down in the dark? Each moment the stillness is its vivid self, both ordinary and miraculous. How can I *not* say thank you?

And is there a something, a someone, to receive my thanks? Is the urge to bow the head simply the recognition of how far forever goes, of how much is unknown, and unknowable? The recognition of the smallness of one human being, and the mystery that attends everything – that attends, so gently, *every single thing?*

This is the day the Lord has made. Here it is, this moment: here it is, as it is. This is it! I am privileged to be here for it. The content of the moment is utterly irrelevant. We don't get to pick and choose the moment the Lord has made. We can piss and moan, or we can rejoice: that we didn't miss it. We were here for it, really here, for every scrap of it.

Rejoice and be glad.

What Doesn't Change

Everything changes. Well, everything in the ordinary world changes. But something doesn't.

A few months ago, I woke in the middle of the night, and as I was coming up through the deep water of unconsciousness into the dark stillness of awareness, I noticed, upon surfacing, that thing I always notice, the primary thing that is continuously palpable. Then I heard a voice say something. It was as if someone were there, observing me awaken, and able to see inside my forming consciousness, and witnessing my noticing that ever-present *something* that underlies and saturates all else.

The voice, as if a head were nodding, said *It's always the same.*

It was as if the thing itself were speaking. Saying *Yes, I'm still here.*

I am not the first to try and fail at describing the nature of that "It." There is a tradition of failed attempts over the millennia. Some heartfelt, some heady. Many impenetrable. But here I go.

It's the continuity, the thing that runs through all. It's what everything has in common. "The ground of being," Krishnamurti called it. When I first came to sense it directly, and without interruption, my impression was that everything seemed to be made of the same stuff. Made of the same material . . . energy . . . *something*. Everything: not just matter (me and you, the painting on the wall, dirt, the car, the warm air), but also life-in-motion. A spoken word, a sensation felt in the body, a series of thoughts in somebody's mind, the flood of sorrow in an aching heart. Effort, directed attention, well meaning, cruelty. All of it elementally kindred.

This "stuff" felt to me like consciousness, somehow – that consciousness was what everything was made out of. Though that word, like the rest of them, is inadequate. Misleading even, as it suggests the ordinary kind of intelligent awareness, the thing that comes alive when you emerge from sleeping.

I've stopped wishing I had a name for it, or even a fathoming. All I know is, it's always here, always itself, in and around everything that goes on. Nothing has the power to draw attention from it. I don't forget. I couldn't possibly not notice its presence. Everything else in awareness is secondary.

Even in the middle of a traumatic event. It is especially noticeable then. I could account for that. Eckhart Tolle already did; I don't need to.

Anyhow, it's just ideas. It's not the thing itself. Like the most vivid, fresh description of the taste of a peach is a light year away from the thing in the mouth.

Everyone is salivating for it. This is what everybody wants. Not just people who call themselves spiritual. There is an intuition that is essentially human, that seems to have come with our equipment, that something runs like a stream below all else – a mode, a place, where rest is absolute. Where the point of existence is a felt thing. Where the thinness of ordinary life concerns is seen through, and it is finally collectively acknowledged that the emperor is unclothed.

Talking to God

Talking to God. Who never talks back. Just a receptivity, a ceaseless openness.

I don't know how to write about this – the thing that's always happening, the most real thing, what saturates awareness more than anything else, day in and day out. Yet no possibility of articulation, putting this into the container of words.

If *this* isn't describable, what's the point of writing at all? Writing about something *sayable* is like looking under the streetlamp for the lost keys, because that's where it's see-able, even though you know the keys were dropped elsewhere.

It's dark here. Not lonely dark, not bereft dark. Not scary. Just wordless. Full of wonder.

The talking to God doesn't happen with words, not mostly. Although sometimes I can't help it. Sometimes the pressure becomes enough that ripening wants that ordinary kind of outlet, that oh-so-human one. "Thank you" will escape my lips, and sometimes "How can this be?"

Walking out the door the first time in a morning, the moist air, the smell of green, the body in fresh receptivity. As if none of it has ever happened before, or been seen, appreciated (the first time since yesterday), the words come out the mouth: "It's still happening!" The cat cradled in my arms takes the breath and the made sounds into his fragrant, sleepy body. I have lowered my lips to the fur at the back of his neck. I am praying to the cat, who is praying to the crook of my arm, where his nostrils are burrowed.

I don't ask God for anything. Not for myself, anyway. Sometimes I say *Bless my children*.

But for myself, there is nothing to ask for. It wouldn't occur to me.

What goes on is more like a mostly unspoken acknowledgment, a recognition of a presence. There isn't anywhere the presence isn't. It's not like me-and-God. It's just . . . *God*. Everywhere and always. And yet . . . yes, there is a recognition, a noticing. Something is here that's capable of awareness. There is an intelligence that notices. A receptivity. A gratitude. A stunned amazement.

Because there is memory of another way. And the mind does a comparison: how it was then, how it is now. Also, how it is in my experience and how it seems to be for others, who are as I have been. Lost in the mind. Unable to notice, or to linger there – to disappear into what gets called God. To be like a little child, or a cat. To not miss the beloved thing.

Here I am, still trying to write about God, about talking to God. God as the smell of a horse, as the feel of olive oil on the fingers, as the softness of the bed when the body is exhausted.

Tear down all the churches, burn the damn scriptures, forget what's in the canons. Don't get bogged down in all that, if it isn't washing you in light. When you take a drink of water, when you've been especially thirsty, make note of the cool, the sensation of traveling over the mysterious interior, the delicious relief. The silence between words. The slick of soap over the skin in the shower. *This* is what we're meant to know: the ordinary miracle of the felt moment. The sensation of aliveness. If this isn't God, well, I don't know. Yes, and even the creaking joints on the stairs. The breaking heart. The ticking of the clock in a room where people are waiting.

All of it.

The Line Dividing Fear From Love

There is a line clearly dividing the first fifty years of life from the years since (twelve, at the present accounting). From here, looking back, it's as if the time before were black-and-white, two-dimensional, a pencil sketch of existence. Though at the time life often appeared (and felt) luxurious, if sometimes tainted with worry and dissatisfaction.

I thought it must be lucky when a writer happened onto the other side of that line, the life-after-death that begins when the mind has grown quiet. When life (no matter the present-moment content) has become sumptuous. A writer, if she tried hard enough, could maybe get somebody's attention, could render paradise vividly enough that no one would be able to turn away from the prospect for themselves. Their own powers of envisioning – sinking into what it would feel like to be constantly peaceful, without angst or fear or loneliness – would engender such a warm and constant presence that longing for all other things would fall away. They'd see that what they could bodily intuit must be innate, within, awaiting discovery.

I used to think if I tried hard enough to describe how things had changed, and if I did it publicly, in a way others could overhear, my account might nudge some to reconsider their lives. To see if life couldn't be lived differently, so sorrow and longing wouldn't saturate them, so frustration and anger would no longer be their bedfellows.

But words (however clear and urgent) are only so useful. They are, after all, part of the problem in the first place. Words, like ideas, are stand-ins for reality. Which means they are frequently in collusion with ego. It's all spun out of the mind, which is so noisy the silence cannot be heard.

* * * * *

I've come to see there's really very little one person can do to inspire what isn't already aching to happen. Someone cares about this or they don't. At least, not enough to make it the centerpiece of attention – without which nothing fundamental will change.

I cannot endow another with that singlepointed focus. It grows all on its own, like a flower or a weed no one planted. It emerges from the dark earth of a person's soul, the quiet of the middle of the night, the airless heart of despair, where nothing is left but giving up. Then there comes the turn toward the flame in the night on the other side of a field, the face in its instinctual turning toward a just-opened window with a little breeze from a direction you never knew was there. That moment is blessed.

Sometimes I attempt to open a window. Strike a match. But maybe no one is there to turn toward the breeze, the flame. Never mind. I can only do what I can do.

Here there are voices insisting – but what a difference a teacher can make, *has* made, when the readiness is there. I see the truth of that. I do what seems possible. I set aside a lot to be with one who is ready to be done with the old way. I will respond, sometimes into the middle of the night. Maybe into old age.

* * * * *

And sometimes – more and more, it seems – there is the expression in someone's eyes, or in the voice, or in the letters on the screen, that says something is happening there. Something radical. The great sweetening is taking over, disassembling so much that seemed to matter, and the original vitality is assuming its rightful place. In the bones, in the gestures, in the work, the play. In perception, in thought (which happens now by choice, no longer by crippling default). Sometimes there is a trembling voice on the phone, eyes filling up in the face of someone sitting just there, and what the person says is some version of this:

I don't know what's happening to me, but God, oh my God.

Nearly always we end up laughing. Amazement has no words. It has laughter, and joy that seems to come in a flood.

I could sit all day and all night, every day for the rest of my sweet life, being in the presence of one (and another and another) who has happened onto the other side of the line dividing fear from love. For that is what it is. That is one way of saying what it is.

When I am in the presence of that, I just want to bow my head. Not to the person exactly but to the miracle of a world where such a thing is able to come about, transformation on such a scale. But I keep my head from bowing, because I don't want to look away. I want to look and look into the blessed eyes of relief, of stunned amazement. Tenderness pooling in those eyes. And why has this person come to sit here? Not because "help" is sought. Such a one no longer wants for anything at all. It's that they have been wandering around unable to explain what's happened, their loved ones looking quizzically at them, maybe in alarm. Or maybe they themselves don't understand what's going on. They want to be with someone they don't have to try to explain anything to. Like seeing in the mirror, that deep looking into the eyes of one who feels the same way.

There are people living their ordinary lives in this quiet amazement. Softness comes into the world wherever they go, whatever they do. Mostly, they are not understood. It doesn't matter. They don't mind not being understood. They don't mind anything at all.

What I Wish for You

Sometimes I ask myself this: *If this were to be my last opportunity to say something that might be of use, what might I say? What would I wish for people?*

That they not miss the moment. Not miss life, the very thing. The now of it. That the mental noise abate enough, some part of every day – some bunch of nows – that they really see, really feel, that they are here. That they are alive, aware of the moment they're in – the moment that *is* what they are. Because all they have of themselves, really, is the deeply personal encounter with this fleeting bit of reality. However much it might seem to be otherwise, however compelling the impression of an ongoing self, having a history and opinions and aspirations (all of which live in the mind, not in life itself).

If I could bring this about for someone, the last time I were to open my mouth or put pen to paper, this is what I would do. It would be enough. Not missing your life is enough. Is abundant. Never mind if you have a big awakening.

But anyway, where else does awakening occur but in the now, in a moment of juicy, sumptuous life? Awareness feeling itself happening, tingly with apprehension of the smell or feel or taste of a thing. Where else but this moment can the revelation occur?

So it's a win-win situation. You may wake up, really wake up: never resist again, never again get lost in thought, or be subject to mind-caused torment, finally knowing what you deeply are. You may not. Probably you won't. Hardly anybody does come to this.

But meanwhile, you won't miss your life! When it comes time to die, you won't have missed the precious thing – the only thing you ever could have had. You'll have paid attention, a good chunk of your allotted time, to what was right in front of you. Good and bad, the pain in the ass, all of it. You won't have failed to pause to feel the wind on your face, to let it mess up your hair. You won't have stopped your heart from breaking, when it needed to break. You'll have allowed yourself to rest, when rest was needed. You won't be sorry it's come time to die.

All you have, or ever will, is *this moment*. It's a jewel in your hand. But briefly, oh so briefly: because here, now, is another. Nothing lasts. You cannot experience anything later (however much your mind might try to get you to). This is the human condition, from which there is no escape. And why would you want to be someplace else? Why see life as being clamped into handcuffs, your fists at your back? There is no solace in fearing what's ahead. Isn't life a feast? It better be. It is restful to be *here,* to really be here, without lament.

In the play *Our Town,* the character known as the stage manager asks the audience this: Does anybody ever live a life fueled by the knowing that something in us is eternal? Not eternal as in outlasting death. Eternal as in not-caught-up-in-time. The stage manager is asking if we feel the ongoing stillness within ourselves, the timeless thing that's devoid of content or motion or trouble of any sort. The now, really felt, is vast and motionless. It goes as far as the sky goes. He is pleading with us to get that, while we're alive.

Feel that, and time isn't a prison. Death isn't a bad guy. Aging isn't an enemy. Every day is your best friend, the most cherished thing, whatever it may bring. A heap of miracles, every one of them imperfect and ordinary and not to be missed. When you stop asking life to "make you happy" – when you sense, at least occasionally, this inner stillness – then life is allowed to be itself, as it comes, moment to moment.

Learn to savor the simple, the plain act that is just itself, without needing to have meaning, without needing to get someplace better. The simple gesture of running the sponge over the soapy plate, a round face without expression. There is no thought for being finished, for the next dish, or for what happens after the dishes are done. Walking up the stairs: just *this* step, this foot on the wood. It's not about getting someplace. The exquisite pleasure of the flex of muscle (even if it's sore), the pressure of the foot against the surface (even if the stairs need repair or sweeping). Even with the body in motion, always there is the stillness.

This is the thing we want. It's how the presence of the eternal is felt to be alive in the ordinary reality of the lived moment. It's not by trying to become different from how you are. It's not (God help us) by trying to wake up! It's about paying attention to what you're doing. Laying a stick of wood onto the fire inside the stove, the feel of the cut surface against fingers and palm. Bending to put the scoop of cat food into the little dish. Pausing to watch the whiskered face lower itself to the fragrant morsel, as if in prayer. (Where do you suppose the cat is, ever, but in this precious moment?)

This is the whole thing. This is it, what life is for. This is the fulfillment, the encounter with the beloved.

Someone asked recently about the meaning of life. *Don't look in the usual places,* I said. If you have to go looking in your head to find some meaning, that isn't it. If there are words for it, that isn't it.

Do you notice what the warm coffee feels like going down your throat? Do you stop to watch the cat enjoy its supper? Did you think it was supposed to be grander than that? What possible "meaning" could come near to feeling yourself be alive?

The best thing that can ever happen is when things stop meaning something. When whatever comes along, or whatever gets done, is left to be its plain self. Unelaborated, unadorned, unnamed. The end of infernal interpretation! The radical relief of it.

In the absence of all that familiar handling, the world floods the scene. Into the open palms come the feet of little birds. Everything is new, as if never seen before. *Thank you* is the only thing left to be said.

* 9 7 8 1 4 5 6 6 2 9 4 5 8 *